JOE BROWN'S

Melange Cafe Cookbook

To Joan

Good cooking

2002

Merry Christmas

Love

Elle

xo xo

JOE BROWN'S

Melange Cafe Cookbook

Joe Brown

small potatoes press

Interior and cover photographs by Donna Connor
Interior design and copy editing by Connie Correia Fisher

Printed in the United States of America
10 9 8 7 6 5 4 3 2 1

Library of Congress Control Number: 2001092668
ISBN: 0-9661200-7-8

Small Potatoes Press
1106 Stokes Avenue
Collingswood, NJ 08108

TO

My father and mother, Paul and France
... may your light forever shine on me ...
who taught me about the important things in life and to always try.

My wife Robin,
for not losing faith in me and for not just being behind me,
but right beside me.

My son Jordan,
for his inspiration and clear understanding
of why I work so hard.

TABLE OF CONTENTS

I have always been the type of person who feels that as long as you are happy, then I am happy too. I think I became a chef because I saw a special look on people's faces after they enjoyed a great meal. That look said "happy" and "satisfied." I realized then that food changes your every emotion. When I found out that I had the ability to do that with food, that I could effect my friends and family in such a positive way, it was then that I fell in love with cooking.

My mother was good at this. When she cooked for us, it was like she knew exactly what we needed, and she delivered in her food. I still smell my mother's yeast rolls and cornbread. My brothers and I would wake up in the middle of the night and sneak downstairs to see if there was just one more piece left. (Keep in mind that I was the youngest of ten kids, so leftovers were a precious commodity!) Often I was too late, and someone else had already beaten me to the punch. The next morning we'd all laugh about who got the goods. No one would confess, but you could always tell who the lucky kid was — the one with crumbs in the bed.

My mom didn't really use recipes. She had learned what worked and what didn't, and she went from there. I go by instinct and experience as well. Recipes are only guidelines, not commandments, so you are welcome to change these recipes and adapt them to your own preferences. When you cook, think about more than taste. Consider texture, appearance, and how all the ingredients work together. And don't forget aroma! Smell is very important. That's why the nose is above the mouth. When something smells good, your taste buds are activated, and you get the full flavor of the food.

Just remember, I have prepared all these dishes the long and complicated way, and I have already made all the mistakes there are to make. You'll see that the recipes are very simple, very easy. There's nothing to be afraid of here. Read the recipe one or two times before you start; get everything together; follow my directions; and most of all, enjoy yourself in the kitchen. Soon you'll see that you can make yourself and your guests very happy. I learned very early in the business that my goal as a chef was to make you happy. That's what my mother and father taught me, and that's what you'll learn from these recipes.

GOOD FOOD MAKES PEOPLE HAPPY.

Joe Brown

PARTY FOODS

Marinated Roasted Red Peppers

SERVES 6 TO 12

When you open a new business, you never know how it will be received. On the opening night of Melange Cafe, I took a deep breath and hoped for the best. I think that was the last time I breathed all evening. We were slammed that night! And the next night and the next. We cook each meal to order, and we struggled to keep up. Won't hurry the cooking ... so to slow people down a bit, I made up this wonderful appetizer that we now serve to each guest. It starts the meal with a bang, although some people say it's a meal in itself.

8 red peppers
1 cup olive oil
½ cup balsamic vinegar
3 tablespoons chopped fresh basil
1 tablespoon chopped fresh garlic
Salt and pepper
1 pound Asiago cheese, sliced into 2-inch-square pieces

Place peppers over an open flame. (Your grill or stove top burner is fine.) Turn occasionally so that all sides are charred. (This might take up to 20 minutes.) Transfer to ice water.

Peel off skins when cool. Remove stems and seeds. Pat dry. Cut peppers into 2-inch-long strips.

Combine remaining ingredients. Add peppers and marinate for at least 1 hour. Serve with great bread and a good bottle of wine or as a plated appetizer over garlic toasts. Keeps refrigerated for up to 7 days.

NOTE: A 28-ounce can of roasted red peppers may be used.

Salmon and Caviar New Potatoes

SERVES 10

This appetizer is a sophisticated (but easy) way to begin a special dinner or party. Keep the potato centers from this recipe for another dish — like garlic mashed potatoes or fried potato patties.

10 new potatoes, scrubbed
6 ounces smoked salmon, sliced
½ cup heavy cream
Salt and pepper to taste
2 ounces caviar

Boil potatoes in salted water until just tender, about 5 to 7 minutes. Drain potatoes and cool slightly.

Preheat broiler. Cut each potato in half lengthwise and hollow out the potato halves, leaving about a ¼-inch thickness. Put potato halves, cut side up, onto a baking dish. Broil until golden and crisp. Remove from oven and reserve.

Combine salmon, heavy cream, and salt and pepper in a food processor. Process until smooth. Use a small spoon to place a dollop of mixture into each potato half. Top each half with caviar. Serve chilled.

Feta Lamb Chops

SERVES 6 TO 8

I come from a big family, so there's always lots of big family parties. Because it gets too crazy if I try to seat everyone for dinner, I usually set up a big buffet and then have a few little stations set up around the house or on the deck. That way no one is ever far from the food, and we don't have to worry about who sits where. These lamb chops are one of the fun finger foods I like to serve.

2 racks of lamb, cut 1-inch thick, bones cleaned of meat or fat
1 pound feta cheese, crumbled
1 teaspoon minced garlic
1 teaspoon dried parsley
1 teaspoon dried oregano
Salt and pepper to taste
1 cup vegetable oil
¼ cup soy sauce
Barbecue sauce (your favorite brand)

Use a sharp knife to make a small slit or pocket in each lamb chop. Fill pockets with approximately ½ teaspoon feta cheese.

Combine garlic, herbs, and salt and pepper and rub over meat. Combine oil, soy sauce, and salt and pepper in a non-reactive bowl large enough to hold the chops. Place chops in bowl, cover, and refrigerate for 1 to 6 hours.

Preheat oven to 350°. Heat a grill or grill pan over medium-high heat. Wipe excess marinade from chops. Sear chops on both sides briefly to mark chops. Brush with a small amount of barbecue sauce. Transfer from grill to oven and bake for 5 to 10 minutes until desired degree of doneness.

Spinach-stuffed Wings
with Red Pepper Sauce

SERVES 4 TO 6

Popeye would be proud of this dish. You'll be proud to serve it at your next casual get together.

1 teaspoon vegetable oil
1 pound spinach, trimmed of stems
1 pound breadcrumbs
½ cup Parmesan cheese
½ cup chicken stock
1 teaspoon minced garlic
Salt and pepper to taste
Joe's Cajun Seasoning to taste (Recipe appears on page 117.)
1 pound fresh chicken wings
6 eggs, beaten
2 cups milk
2 cups flour
6 cups frying oil (or enough to cover chicken when frying)
1 teaspoon red pepper flakes
½ cup honey
¼ cup Dijon mustard

Heat vegetable oil in a large sauté pan. Add spinach, ½ cup breadcrumbs, Parmesan cheese, stock, garlic, salt, pepper, and Joe's Cajun Seasoning. Sauté until mixture is thick. Remove from heat and let cool.

Meanwhile, butterfly each wing lengthwise and expose the bone. Cut through joint below the wing bone (the top bone) and remove all bones, except wing tip, leaving meat and skin intact. Reserve.

Stuff each wing with spinach mixture. Close to seal. Season chicken with salt, pepper, and Joe's Cajun Seasoning to taste. Beat together eggs and milk. In a separate bowl, season flour with salt, pepper, and Joe's Cajun Seasoning to taste. Roll chicken in seasoned flour, dip in egg wash, then dredge in remaining breadcrumbs.

Heat oil in a large frying pan to 350°. Place chicken in hot oil and fry until brown and coked through. Keep warm.

Combine red pepper flakes, honey, and Dijon mustard in a saucepan over medium heat. Bring to a simmer, then remove from heat. Toss wings with sauce or serve as a dipping sauce.

Crawfish Stuffed Wontons
with Red Pepper Honey Mustard Reduction

SERVES 6 TO 8

I really like this fusion of Chinese wontons and Cajun crawfish. Serve as a first course appetizer, a passed hors d'oeuvre, or a fun snack.

- **1 cup water**
- **1 cup cooked and peeled crawfish meat**
- **¼ cup chopped green pepper**
- **¼ cup chopped onion**
- **2 tablespoons mayonnaise**
- **1 tablespoon Worcestershire sauce**
- **1 tablespoon Old Bay Seasoning**
- **½ tablespoon Joe's Cajun Seasoning** **(Recipe appears on page 117.)**
- **½ teaspoon chopped fresh garlic**
- **24 prepared wontons skins (4 x 4 inches each)**
- **2 cups soy oil**
- **Red Pepper Honey Mustard Reduction (see recipe)**

Combine all ingredients, except skins and oil, and reserve.

Lay out a wonton skin on a cool working surface. Place 1 tablespoon filling in center of wonton. Fold wonton in half to form a triangle. Mend edges with water and seal with a fork. Reserve on wax paper. Continue with remaining stuffing and skins.

Refrigerate until ready to fry.

Heat oil to 350°. Fry wontons, a few at a time, about 2 minutes per side, until crisp and golden. Drain on paper towel. Serve immediately with reduction.

Red Pepper Honey Mustard Reduction

Great with smoked shrimp or over fresh spinach and mushrooms.

½ cup honey
½ cup mustard
1 tablespoon red pepper flakes

Combine all ingredients in a medium saucepan. Bring to a boil over medium heat. Reduce heat and simmer for 3 minutes.

Serve as a dipping sauce or on top of wontons.

Grilled Shrimp
with Pecan Corn Crab Relish

SERVES 4

This is a wonderful buffet or picnic dish. You'll love the crunch and vibrant flavors. It's amazingly easy too! Relish and shrimp may be prepared up to one day in advance.

1 pound large (16-20 size) shrimp, peeled and deveined
8 ounces jumbo lump crabmeat
1 cup pecan halves
1 cup cooked corn kernels
1 cup diced scallions
4 tablespoons diced roasted red pepper
4 tablespoons chopped parsley
2 lemons
Salt and black pepper
Lemon Butter Sauce, optional (see recipe)

Heat grill or grill pan to high. Grill shrimp, about 2 minutes per side, until white. Let cool and reserve.

Combine crabmeat, pecans, corn, scallions, red pepper, and parsley. Squeeze on lemon juice. Season with salt and pepper. Toss to combine.

Place relish in the middle of a bowl or serving plate. Top with shrimp. Serve cold or at room temperature with or without lemon sauce.

NOTE: Chicken can be substituted for shrimp. Cut 1 pound boneless chicken breasts into 3-inch tenders. Heat grill or grill pan to high. Grill chicken for 3 minutes on each side or until cooked through.

Lemon Butter Sauce

Juice of 4 lemons
¾ cup white wine
12 tablespoons cold butter, cubed

Combine lemon juice and wine in a saucepan. Cook over high heat until reduced by one-third. Add butter, a little at a time, whisking constantly until emulsified. Serve immediately.

Muffuletta Bruschetta

SERVES A CROWD

Muffuletta is New Orleans' answer to the hero, sub, or as we call it in South Jersey, the hoagie. Traditionally, it consists of a split round roll filled with sliced provolone cheese, Genoa salami, and ham topped with pickled olive salad. The olive salad and sandwich were invented by Signor Lupo Salvadore in 1906 at the Central Grocery on Decatur Street. You can still buy the sandwich and salad there, but why not try this homemade version at your next party.

1 cup pitted Spanish green olives
1 cup pitted kalamata olives
¼ cup chopped red onion
2 tablespoons chopped fresh basil
2 tablespoons lemon juice
1 tablespoon grated horseradish
1 tablespoon chopped garlic
1 tablespoon Dijon mustard
1 teaspoon Worcestershire sauce
Dash of hot sauce
½ cup plus 2 tablespoons olive oil
Salt and pepper
1 loaf sourdough or French bread

Combine first 10 ingredients in a food processor and process until coarse. With processor running, gradually add ½ cup olive oil. Transfer mixture to a bowl. Season to taste with salt and pepper. Cover and refrigerate for at least 1 hour. (Mixture may be kept refrigerated for up to 24 hours.)

Heat grill or broiler. Cut bread on an angle into ¼-inch-thick slices. Brush each slice with remaining oil. Grill or broil bread slices until just crisp. Season with pepper.

Top each slice with olive mixture and serve.

JOE'S KITCHEN

APPETIZERS AND SALADS

Fried Cheese Grit Cakes
with Crawfish Creole Sauce

SERVES 4

One day, a regular customer made a special request for grits. So I made up a big batch of cheesy grits. The way they firmed up sort of reminded me of polenta, an Italian way of preparing corn meal. So in Melange fusion fashion, I gave a Southern staple an Italian–Creole twist. Grits . . . they're not just for breakfast anymore!

2 cups water
½ cup instant grits
4 ounces Cheddar or American cheese, shredded
Dash of garlic powder
2 cups soy oil
Crawfish Creole Sauce (see recipe)

Bring water to a boil in a saucepan. Slowly stir in grits. Reduce heat to medium-low. Cover and cook, stirring occasionally, for 5 to 7 minutes. Stir in cheese and garlic powder. Cook until cheese melts, about 2 to 3 minutes.

Pour hot grits into a 9 x 12-inch cookie pan. Spread to cover bottom of pan. Refrigerate until firm. Cut into 2 x 2-inch squares or triangles. Refrigerate until ready to fry.

Heat oil in a skillet over high heat to 350°. Add grit cakes, a few at a time. Fry until brown on each side, roughly 2 minutes. Drain on paper towel.

Place on serving platter and top with sauce.

Crawfish Creole Sauce

This is my version of the classic Creole Marinara. Thick and chunky with big bites of veggies and crawfish, it's a satisfying sauce to serve over pasta, chicken, seafood, and – as you see – grit cakes.

1 tablespoon soy oil
½ cup diced onion
½ cup diced celery
½ cup diced green pepper
1 teaspoon chopped fresh garlic
1 can (16 ounces) peeled plum tomatoes
1 cup chicken stock
1 cup cooked and peeled whole crawfish
1 tablespoon Joe's Cajun Seasoning **(Recipe appears on page 117.)**
½ teaspoon black pepper
1 teaspoon thyme
1 tablespoon cornstarch
2 tablespoons cold water
Salt

Heat oil in a large skillet over medium-high heat. Add onion, celery, green pepper, and garlic. Sauté until onions are translucent.

Add tomatoes, stock, and crawfish. Bring to a simmer. Stir in Joe's Cajun Seasoning, black pepper, and thyme.

Combine cornstarch and water. Stir into sauce to thicken. Season to taste with salt.

Fried Oysters

with Horseradish Mustard Reduction and Tomato-Corn Relish

SERVES 4

I had the pleasure of preparing this dish for Susan Powell, host of the "Home Matters" television show. I thought this would be a fun recipe for the TV audience to try. I knew that Ms. Powell loves hot and spicy foods so when the cameras rolled, I added an extra kick of horseradish to the reduction just for her. The result? I was asked to reappear on the show next season!

24 large oysters

1 cup flour

2 tablespoons Joe's Cajun Seasoning (Recipe appears on page 117.)

2 eggs

1 cup milk

1 cup corn meal

2 cups breadcrumbs

½ cup oil

Salt

Horseradish Mustard Reduction (see recipe)

2 cups Tomato-Corn Relish (see recipe)

Shuck oysters and set aside.

Combine flour and 1 tablespoon Joe's Cajun Seasoning in a small bowl. Whisk together eggs and milk in a separate bowl. Combine corn meal and breadcrumbs in a third bowl. Dip oysters in flour and then in egg wash. Dredge oysters in corn meal mixture and tap off excess. Refrigerate until ready to cook.

Heat oil in a large skillet over high heat. When oil is hot, gently add oysters and fry until golden brown, about 1½ minutes per side. Remove and drain on paper towels. Sprinkle with salt.

Coat the bottoms of 4 serving plates with horseradish mustard reduction. Arrange 6 oysters around the edges of each plate like the spokes on a wheel. Place a mound of relish in the center. Serve immediately.

Horseradish Mustard Reduction

1 cup horseradish
1 cup Dijon mustard
2 cups heavy cream

Combine all ingredients in a saucepan over medium-high heat. Bring to a boil. Reduce heat and simmer, whisking gently until mixture reduces slightly and is thick enough to coat the back of a spoon without running off. Serve immediately.

Tomato-Corn Relish

4 ripe tomatoes, peeled and diced
¼ cup blanched corn kernels
¼ cup minced onion
1 teaspoon minced jalapeño peppers
2 tablespoons chopped parsley
1 tablespoon freshly squeezed lime juice
1 teaspoon freshly squeezed lemon juice
½ teaspoon salt
4 turns freshly ground black pepper

Combine all ingredients in a bowl and stir gently to combine. Prepare at least 30 minutes before serving so that flavors can marry.

Shrimp Rémoulade

SERVES 4

Rémoulade is a classic mayonnaise-based sauce. Originally from France, it has been adopted by New Orleans chefs – who spice the basic recipe up with Creole mustard – and can be found in just about every restaurant in South Louisiana.

2 pounds jumbo shrimp, deveined
⅓ cup finely diced green onions
⅓ cup finely diced celery
¼ cup finely chopped parsley
1 tablespoon minced garlic
1½ cups mayonnaise
¼ cup Creole mustard
1 tablespoon Worcestershire sauce
2 teaspoons lemon juice
1 teaspoon Tabasco sauce
1 tablespoon paprika
Salt and pepper to taste
1 head Romaine lettuce, chopped

In a large stockpot, bring to a boil enough water to cover shrimp. Add shrimp. Boil for 5 to 8 minutes. Drain and chill. Peel when cool enough to handle. Chill until ready to serve.

Combine remaining ingredients, except lettuce, in a mixing bowl and combine well. Cover and refrigerate for at least 4 hours before serving.

To serve, divide lettuce between four plates. Top with shrimp and then with a generous dollop of sauce.

Not Really Barbecued Shrimp

SERVES 4 TO 6

There are countless variations of barbecued shrimp on French Quarter menus. Funny thing is, none of the recipes call for a barbecue pit or grill. What they DO call for is an outrageous amount of butter. Don't skimp on it: you can diet tomorrow. It's the New Orleans way.

5 pounds shrimp, unpeeled
2 pounds butter
5 cloves garlic, minced
1 medium onion, minced
3 ribs celery, minced
¾ cup beer
½ cup Worcestershire sauce
2 teaspoons lemon juice
4 tablespoons chopped fresh parsley
2 tablespoons chopped fresh rosemary
2 tablespoons Joe's Cajun Seasoning **(Recipe appears on page 117.)**
French bread

Wash shrimp and spread them out in shallow baking pans. Reserve.

Melt butter over medium heat. Add garlic, onion, and celery and sauté until onion is translucent. Add remaining ingredients, except bread. Pour over shrimp. Refrigerate several hours, basting and turning shrimp every 30 minutes.

Preheat oven to 300°. Bake for 30 minutes, turning every 10 minutes, until shrimp turn pink.

Ladle shrimp and butter sauce into large soup bowls. Serve with French bread for dipping.

Curried Coconut Shrimp

SERVES 4

We served this dish for our Halloween celebration which featured "Chef Brown's Original New Orleans Voodoo Cuisine." Voodoo Cuisine – created especially for the bash – builds on our year-round menu of Louisiana and Italian fusion by mixing in Haitian, West African, Caribbean, and French-Creole flavors and cultural Halloween connections. The hallmark of Haitian cooking is the use of a spice blend that includes fresh garlic, cloves, thyme, and a variety of Scotch bonnet peppers.

- ¼ cup soy oil
- 2 pounds large shrimp, peeled and deveined
- 2 cloves garlic, finely chopped
- 1 red bell pepper, seeded and finely chopped
- 1 Scotch bonnet chile, seeded and finely chopped
- 1 tablespoon mild curry powder
- 2 cups coconut milk
- Salt and pepper to taste
- 1 bunch cilantro leaves, finely chopped
- Sweet Potato Fries, optional (Recipe appears on page 85.)

Heat oil in a heavy-bottomed saucepan over medium heat. Add shrimp, garlic, bell pepper, and Scotch bonnet chile. Cook for 3 to 4 minutes. Stir in curry powder and cook 1 minute.

Add coconut milk and salt and pepper to taste. Increase heat to high. Cook for about 10 minutes, stirring constantly, until sauce is thick and reduced.

Garnish with cilantro leaves and serve with sweet potato fries, if you like.

Steamed Crawfish

SERVES 4

Ever been to a crawfish boil? It's a foot stompin', lip smackin', mosquito whackin', alligator dodgin' good time! This is my version of a boil, minus the alligators.

48 whole fresh crawfish (Frozen may be substituted.)
1 bottle (12 ounces) dark beer
4 cups water or fish stock
2 tablespoons chopped fresh garlic
2 tablespoons Old Bay Seasoning
1 teaspoon cayenne pepper
2 teaspoons kosher or sea salt
½ teaspoon black pepper

Clean crawfish and reserve.

Combine remaining ingredients in a large stockpot and bring to a boil. Add crawfish and cover. Boil for 6 to 10 minutes or until crawfish shells are bright red. Remove crawfish. Arrange on a serving platter and reserve.

Strain broth. Measure out 3 cups and return to stockpot. Reheat over medium heat. Taste and adjust seasonings. Pour broth over crawfish and serve.

Crabmeat Cheesecake
with Wild Mushroom and Onion Sauté

YIELDS 14 2-INCH WEDGES

Crabmeat cheesecake? No, that's not a typo. I created this savory recipe after a trip to New Orleans, and it's become one of our best sellers. We must make a dozen a week. If you make just one, your friends and family will sing your praises. Serve it hot or at room temperature as an appetizer, lunch or brunch entree, or on a buffet.

- **3 cups flour**
- **3 cups pecans**
- **½ pound unsalted cold butter, diced small**
- **½ cup cold water**
- **½ cup minced onions or shallots**
- **1½ pounds cream cheese, cubed**
- **7 large eggs**
- **1 teaspoon salt**
- **½ cup hot sauce (vary according to your preference)**
- **½ cup Worcestershire sauce**
- **1 pound jumbo lump crabmeat, picked clean**
- **1 pound lump crabmeat, picked clean**
- **Wild Mushroom and Onion Sauté (see recipe)**

Preheat oven to 350°. Place flour and pecans in a food processor and pulse to combine. Add butter, a little at a time, and pulse until clumps form and mixture binds together. Transfer to a large mixing bowl. Add water, 1 tablespoon at a time, and mix with hands until dough binds together. (You may not need all the water.)

Press dough into bottom and up sides of a 10 x 3-inch springform pan. (Depending on how thick you make your crust, you may have some crust leftover.) Bake in oven, about 15 to 20 minutes, until crust starts to brown. Reserve.

Meanwhile, sauté onions until translucent. Reserve.

Place cream cheese, eggs, salt, hot sauce, and Worcestershire in a food processor and blend until combined. Transfer to a mixing bowl. Gently fold in sautéed onions and crabmeat. Do not overwork.

Pour mixture into baked crust. Bake for 90 to 100 minutes or until top is well browned and an inserted knife comes out clean. (Your oven may vary.) Cut into wedges. Serve alone or with wild mushroom and onion sauté.

Wild Mushroom and Onion Sauté

¼ cup unsalted butter
1 cup sliced white onions
1 cup sliced shiitake or other wild mushrooms
½ cup fresh lemon juice
¼ cup Worcestershire sauce
¼ cup hot sauce
1½ cups heavy cream
4 ounces jumbo lump crabmeat or crab claws
Salt and pepper to taste

Melt butter in a large sauté pan over high heat. Add onions and mushrooms. Cook until onions are translucent. Add lemon juice, Worcestershire, hot sauce, and cream. Cook until mixture is thick and liquid is reduced by half. Add crabmeat or claws and gently stir to combine. Cook until heated through. Serve over cheesecake slices.

Caesar Salad

SERVES 4

Two things make a great Caesar salad: well-chilled, dry romaine lettuce and lots of good quality Parmesan cheese. Serve some extra cheese on the side for extra zing.

- 2 heads romaine lettuce, cored
- 6 egg yolks
- 1 cup olive oil
- 1 tablespoon chopped fresh garlic
- 2 tablespoons Worcestershire sauce
- 1 tablespoon prepared mustard (I like Grey Poupon.)
- 1 tablespoon dried oregano
- ¾ cup freshly grated Parmesan cheese
- ½ cup minced anchovies
- Juice of 1 lemon
- ½ cup red wine vinegar
- Freshly ground black pepper
- Shaved Parmesan
- Easy Croutons (see recipe)

Wash and dry romaine leaves. Tear into bite-size pieces and chill.

Whisk together yolks and oil until emulsified (thick and satiny). Add garlic, Worcestershire, mustard, oregano, grated Parmesan, anchovies, lemon juice, and vinegar (in that order), whisking continuously until well combined.

Toss lettuce with dressing. Season to taste with freshly ground black pepper. Top with shaved Parmesan and croutons.

Easy Croutons

This is such a simple recipe that ingredient amounts are really not needed. Use the suggested amounts listed below as a guideline; then toss, taste, and enjoy!

4 slices stale bread, cubed
3 tablespoons oil or clarified butter
2 to 4 teaspoons Parmesan cheese
1 teaspoon dried oregano
Salt and pepper to taste

Preheat oven to 350°. Toss bread with oil. Add remaining ingredients and toss again. Lay on a sheet pan. Bake in oven until brown. Serve hot or at room temperature. Croutons will last 7 days in a covered container.

Spinach Salad
with Honey Mustard Vinaigrette

SERVES 4

Besides being great on salads, Honey-Mustard Dressing is a fine pre-grill marinade or even a dipping sauce for French fries (think about it – doesn't that sound good?).Use this recipe as the basis for a salad entrée; add grilled vegetables (zucchini, tomatoes, onions, eggplant or asparagus), your favorite cheese, hard-cooked eggs or cooked meats. The choices are unlimited!

- 1 cup honey
- ½ cup prepared mustard (I like Grey Poupon.)
- ½ cup minced yellow onion
- 1 cup balsamic vinegar
- 2 cups extra virgin olive oil
- Salt and pepper
- 16 ounces fresh baby spinach
- ½ pound bacon, cooked and crumbled
- 1 red onion, sliced thinly
- 1 cup Easy Croutons (Recipe appears on page 33.)

Whisk together honey, mustard, yellow onion, and vinegar Gradually add oil, whisking until mixture emulsifies (becomes thick and satiny). Season to taste with salt and pepper. Refrigerate until ready to serve and up to 10 days.

Toss spinach, bacon, and onion in large bowl. Drizzle with vinaigrette. Top with croutons.

Arugula and Candied Walnuts
with Raspberry Vinaigrette

SERVES 4

The peppery mustard flavor of arugula is a nice contrast to the sweet vinaigrette and candied walnuts. If you don't have time to make the candied walnuts, just toast plain walnuts for a few minutes.

2 tablespoons vegetable oil
2 tablespoons sugar
2 tablespoons honey
½ cup walnut halves
2 tablespoons raspberry jam
1 tablespoon raspberry vinegar
1 tablespoon minced shallot
2 tablespoons olive oil
1½ teaspoons walnut oil
Salt and pepper
2 bunches arugula, trimmed
¼ cup chopped mixed dried fruit
½ cup crumbled blue cheese

Heat vegetable oil in a heavy skillet over medium heat. Add sugar and honey and stir until sugar dissolves. Add walnuts and stir until coated. Continue stirring until walnuts are toasted. Transfer walnuts to a foil-lined sheet pan and cool.

Combine jam, vinegar, and shallot in a bowl. Slowly whisk in oils until emulsified. Season to taste with salt and pepper.

Combine arugula, walnuts, and dried fruit and toss with vinaigrette. Top with blue cheese.

Pear and Pecan Salad
with Gorgonzola Vinaigrette

SERVES 4

You see the term "mesclun" on every restaurant menu nowadays. It is a fancy term for assorted seasonal greens and lettuce seedlings that are ready to serve. You can find it at most grocery stores, sometimes labeled as "spring mix." Baby greens work well, too.

6 eggs yolks
1 cup extra virgin olive oil or blended oil
1 cup crumbled Gorgonzola cheese or blue cheese
½ cup red wine vinegar
¼ cup water
¼ cup chopped fresh parsley
1 tablespoon chopped fresh garlic
1 tablespoon dried oregano
Salt and pepper
12 ounces mesclun or mixed salad greens
1 pear, cored and sliced
½ cup seedless red grapes, halved
¼ cup pecan halves

Whisk together egg yolks and oil until emulsifies (becomes thick and satiny). Whisk in Gorgonzola, vinegar, water, parsley, garlic, oregano, and salt and pepper to taste. Refrigerate until ready to serve and up to 4 days. (The flavor intensifies as it sits.)

Toss mesclun, pears and grapes in large bowl. Drizzle with dressing. Top with pecans just before serving.

NOTE: Because they contain lecithin, eggs are natural emulsifiers. They are used to help thicken the dressing and bind together the oil and water, two normally noncombinative substances. For safety reasons, use only fresh eggs, maintained at 40° or less, to ensure that bacteria does not develop.

Lamb Salad
with Brown's Balsamic Dressing

SERVES 4

This recipe is so simple that it demands you to take the ingredients seriously. Take the time to select perfect chops and tomatoes. Cut the potatoes into evenly sized shoestrings. Carefully wash and dry the greens. You'll be rewarded with a meal that's simply sensational.

¼ cup balsamic vinegar
1 teaspoon chopped fresh garlic
1 teaspoon fresh or ½ teaspoon dried oregano
½ cup extra virgin olive oil
Salt and pepper
16 baby lamb chops (about 2 to 3 ounces each)
4 Idaho potatoes, cut into shoestrings
4 cups soy oil
Salt and pepper
1 pound mesclun or mixed greens, washed and dried
2 tomatoes, cut into eighths
1 cucumber, cut into 16 slices

Whisk together vinegar, garlic, and oregano. Gradually add oil, whisking until mixture emulsifies. Season to taste with salt and pepper. Refrigerate until ready to serve and up to 10 days.

Heat grill or grill pan to medium-high heat. Grill lamb chops approximately 2 minutes per side or until desired doneness. Reserve.

Heat oil in a deep fryer or heavy-bottomed pan to 350°. Add potatoes and fry to golden brown, about 4 minutes. Drain on paper towel. Season with salt and pepper and reserve.

Toss greens with dressing. Divide among 4 plates. Cover greens with chops and shoestring fries. Garnish with tomatoes and cucumbers.

Crab Cake Salad
with Tomato-Basil Dressing

SERVES 4

Searching for a special luncheon salad? You've found it in this crowd-pleasing classic that also works well as a light supper or an elegant appetizer.

- **12 ounces jumbo lump crabmeat, picked clean**
- **2 tablespoons breadcrumbs**
- **2 tablespoons chopped fresh parsley**
- **¼ cup mayonnaise**
- **1 tablespoon Worcestershire sauce**
- **½ tablespoon Old Bay Seasoning**
- **½ tablespoon Dijon mustard**
- **1 cup flour**
- **½ cup yellow corn meal**
- **2 cups soy oil**
- **2 leeks, white part only, well washed and finely julienned**
- **1 pound mesclun or mixed greens, washed and dried**
- **16 red or yellow grape tomatoes**
- **Tomato-Basil Dressing (see recipe)**
- **Garlic Toasts (see recipe)**

Combine crabmeat, breadcrumbs, parsley, mayonnaise, Worcestershire, Old Bay, and mustard. Form into 4 patties. Combine flour and corn meal. Lightly dust cakes with flour mixture and set aside.

Heat oil to 350° in a large skillet over medium-high heat. Add cakes and sauté for approximately 2 minutes on each side or until golden brown. Drain on paper towel and reserve.

Reheat oil to 350°. Fry leeks until crispy but not burned. Drain on paper towel and reserve.

Toss greens and tomatoes with dressing and divide among 4 plates. Top each with a crab cake. Garnish with leeks and garlic toasts.

Tomato-Basil Dressing

- **1½ cups chopped fresh plum tomatoes**
- **¼ cup basil, chiffonade (cut into thin strips)**
- **2 tablespoons chopped fresh garlic**
- **2 tablespoons minced onion**
- **½ cup balsamic vinegar**
- **Juice of ½ lime**
- **1 cup extra virgin olive oil**
- **Salt and pepper**

Combine all ingredients, except oil and salt and pepper. Gradually add oil, whisking until mixture is well blended. Season to taste with salt and pepper. Refrigerate until ready to serve and up to 7 days.

Garlic Toasts

- **1 loaf good French bread**
- **½ cup butter**
- **1 tablespoon grated Parmesan cheese**
- **1 teaspoon chopped fresh garlic**
- **1 teaspoon dried oregano**
- **¼ cup extra virgin olive oil**

Preheat oven to 350°. Cut bread on a bias into sixteen ½-inch-thick slices. Reserve.

Combine butter, Parmesan, garlic, and oregano in food processor. Gradually add oil and pulse until well combined. Spread mixture on bread slices. Place on baking sheet. Bake until crispy and brown, about 5 minutes.

Fried Crawfish Salad
with Tomato-Leek Vinaigrette

SERVES 4

I like the ying and yang of this salad: the way the crispy crawfish plays off the delicate texture of the greens and the softness of the cheese. It makes for an elegant summer entree or a substantial first course.

3 cups chopped ripe Jersey tomatoes
¼ cup minced onion or shallot
2 tablespoons minced fresh garlic
2 leeks,white part only, julienned
2 tablespoons chopped fresh basil
Juice of 1 lime
½ cup balsamic vinegar
1 cup extra virgin olive oil
Salt and pepper to taste
3 eggs
1 cup milk
1 pound cooked and peeled crawfish
1 cup flour
2 cups breadcrumbs
1 pound mesclun or salad greens
6 cups soy oil
2 cups crumbled Gorgonzola

Combine first 7 ingredients in a bowl. Slowly whisk in oil until vinaigrette is emulsified. Season with salt and pepper to taste. Refrigerate until ready to serve and up to 7 days.

Whisk together eggs and milk. Dip crawfish in flour and then in egg wash. Dredge crawfish in breadcrumbs and tap off excess. Refrigerate until ready to cook.

Toss mesclun with vinaigrette to taste. Divide among 4 plates. Refrigerate.

Heat oil to 350° in a large cast-iron pan or mini fryer. Carefully place crawfish in oil and fry until golden brown, about 5 minutes. Remove and drain on paper towels. Immediately place crawfish on mesclun and top with crumbled cheese.

Fried Green Tomato Salad
with Shrimp Rémoulade

SERVES 4

This recipe combines two of my favorite things: cool, tangy, shrimp rémoulade and hot, crunchy, fried green tomatoes. Fried green tomatoes are a classic low country Southern dish. Combined with shrimp rémoulade, they get city slicker style.

4 large green tomatoes
1 cup flour
1 teaspoon salt
2 large eggs
½ cup milk
¼ teaspoon Tabasco sauce
1 cup cornmeal
2 tablespoons grated Parmesan cheese
¼ cup olive oil
¼ cup butter
Salt and freshly ground pepper
1 head Romaine lettuce, chopped
Shrimp Rémoulade (Recipe appears on page 26.)

Cut tomatoes into thick slices and discard ends.

Mix together flour and salt in a shallow bowl. Whisk together eggs, milk, and Tabasco in a second bowl. In a third bowl, combine cornmeal and Parmesan cheese.

Dredge each tomato slice in flour (tapping off excess), then dip in egg wash, and coat with cornmeal.

Heat a large heavy skillet over medium heat. Heat oil and butter in pan. Fry tomatoes until golden on both sides. (Do not overcrowd. Fry in batches if pan is not big enough.) Drain on paper towel. Season with salt and freshly ground pepper.

Divide lettuce between four plates. Cover with slices of hot fried tomatoes.Top with shrimp and then a generous dollop of sauce.

Red Bliss Potato Crab Salad

SERVES 4

Crabmeat adds a little twist to the traditional German potato salad. Although this is a perfect side dish for any picnic, I like to serve it as a casual main course, adding romaine lettuce and slices of Jersey tomato and avocado.

6 to 8 red bliss potatoes, skin on
½ cup chopped onion
1 to 2 teaspoons dried parsley
¼ cup red wine vinegar
¼ cup olive oil
½ cup warm chicken stock
1 teaspoon sugar
1 cup jumbo lump crabmeat, picked clean
Salt and pepper

Cook potatoes in boiling water until fork-tender, about 12 to 15 minutes. Strain and cool. Slice when cool enough to handle.

Combine remaining ingredients, except crabmeat and salt and pepper, in a bowl. Mix in potato slices. Gently fold in crabmeat and season with salt and pepper. Serve immediately or refrigerate and serve chilled.

Asparagus and Crab Salad

SERVES 2 AS APPETIZER OR LUNCH ENTREE

There is a certain time of year in New Jersey when tomatoes, asparagus, and crabs run wild. This salad walks on the wild side and leads me back to my early Jersey summers.

2 large red bliss potatoes, skins on
1 medium yellow onion, peeled and sliced into ½-inch-thick rounds
½ cup sliced shiitake mushrooms, stems removed
1 pound asparagus, ends trimmed
10 red grape tomatoes, halved
10 yellow grape tomatoes, halved
½ cup pitted kalamata olives
½ cup extra virgin olive oil
Juice of 1 lemon
½ teaspoon garlic
Salt and pepper to taste
1 pound jumbo lump crabmeat, picked clean

Boil potatoes in salted water until fork tender, about 20 minutes. Cool and slice into ¼-inch rounds.

Grill onion until translucent. Remove from grill and cool.

Cook shiitake mushrooms in boiling water for 30 seconds. Drain and cool.

Boil asparagus in salted water for 2 minutes. Cool in ice cold water and drain.

Combine all ingredients, except crabmeat. Gently toss mixture with crabmeat. Serve immediately at room temperature.

SOUPS AND STEWS

Summer Gazpacho
with Marinated Crawfish

SERVES 4

Even on the hottest summer day, this soup is sure to please. Cool and refreshing, the inclusion of crawfish makes it perfect for a light supper or a nourishing lunch. Marinated crawfish is a wonderful garnish for any salad or pasta. Or you can just eat them as is, which is my favorite way!

6 tablespoons balsamic vinegar
4 tablespoons extra virgin olive oil
1 clove garlic, chopped
Salt and pepper
4 ounces cooked and peeled crawfish meat
1 pound plum tomatoes, peeled and seeded
1 cup plus 2 tablespoons peeled, seeded, and diced cucumber
½ cup minced onion
½ cup diced fennel
¼ cup plus 2 tablespoons diced red bell pepper
1 tablespoon chopped garlic
½ cup chicken stock
1 tablespoon tomato paste
Dash of Tabasco sauce
1 tablespoon chopped fresh tarragon

Combine 4 tablespoons balsamic vinegar, 2 tablespoons olive oil, garlic, and salt and pepper to taste. Toss with crawfish meat. Chill overnight.

In a separate bowl, combine remaining balsamic vinegar and olive oil. Add all remaining ingredients. Puree with a hand blender or in a food processor until smooth. Chill overnight.

Serve soup cold, garnished with marinated crawfish.

Joe Knows Chicken Noodle Soup

SERVES 8

Everyone needs a great, basic chicken soup recipe. Joe knows this, and he delivers with a creation that is foolproof.

1 whole chicken (2 pounds)
2½ quarts water
½ cup medium diced carrot
½ cup medium diced celery
½ cup medium diced onion
2 cups firmly packed fresh chopped spinach
1 cup chopped tomatoes
1 tablespoon chopped fresh garlic
1 tablespoon chopped fresh basil
1 cup uncooked pasta (I like to use tortellini.)
Salt and pepper
¼ cup grated Parmesan cheese

Remove skin from chicken. Place chicken in a large stockpot. Pour in water (add more water if chicken is not completely covered) and bring to a boil. Reduce heat and simmer for 1½ hours. Remove chicken from pot and reserve stock. Let chicken stand until cool enough to handle. Pick off meat and reserve. Discard bones and any remaining skin.

Strain stock and return to stockpot. (If stock measures less than 2 quarts, add some canned chicken broth.) Add vegetables, herbs, and pasta to the pot. Bring to a boil. Reduce heat and simmer for 15 minutes.

Season with salt and pepper. Add chicken and simmer until chicken is heated through. Stir in Parmesan cheese. Taste and adjust seasoning.

NOTE: You may substitute 1 pound chicken breast halves for whole chicken.

Okra Soup

SERVES 4

Okra is the mainstay of the African table and is featured prominently in soups, such as this one which we featured during Black History Month.

- **1 yellow onion, finely chopped**
- **4 tomatoes, seeded and chopped**
- **1 fresh red or green chile, finely chopped**
- **¼ pound dried smoked fish or dried shrimp**
- **6 cups water**
- **1 tablespoon minced fresh ginger**
- **Salt and pepper**
- **½ globe eggplant, cut into ½-inch cubes**
- **½ pound okra, cut into ½-inch-thick rounds**
- **½ pound crabmeat, picked clean**
- **2 tablespoons red palm oil, optional**

Combine onion, tomatoes, chile, dried fish, water, and ginger in a heavy saucepan. Heat over medium-high heat. Bring to a boil.

Reduce heat to medium and simmer, uncovered, about 10 minutes. Season with salt and pepper to taste.

Stir in eggplant and cook until tender, about 6 to 8 minutes. Add okra and crabmeat and cook another 5 minutes or until okra is tender. Stir in palm oil. Taste and adjust seasoning.

Joe's Pumpkin Soup

SERVES 4

Don't reserve this recipe just for Halloween. It's a real treat whenever you want a warm and comforting bowl of soup.

- 2 quarts chicken stock
- 2 cups pureed pumpkin
- 1 cup firmly packed chopped spinach
- ¼ cup chopped onion
- ¼ cup chopped celery
- ¼ cup chopped carrot
- 1 teaspoon chopped fresh garlic
- 1 teaspoon curry
- 1 teaspoon cumin
- 1 teaspoon sugar
- 1 teaspoon cinnamon
- ¼ cup heavy cream
- Salt and pepper to taste
- Crème fraîche or sour cream, optional
- Toasted pumpkin seeds, optional

Combine all ingredients, except salt and pepper and garnishes, in a large stockpot and bring to a boil. Reduce heat and simmer until thick, about 10 minutes. Season to taste with salt and pepper.

Serve topped with a dollop of crème fraîche and a sprinkle of toasted pumpkin seeds.

Crawfish Potato Corn Chowder

SERVES 4

I just got tired of making the same old chowder. Anybody can do that. This — I think — takes chowder to a whole new level. Try it and tell me what you think.

- 2 potatoes, peeled and diced
- 2 ears fresh corn (Frozen corn can be substituted if fresh is not available.)
- ½ cup diced celery
- ½ cup diced green pepper
- ½ cup diced onion
- 3 cups chicken stock
- 1½ cups whole peeled crawfish
- ¼ teaspoon cayenne pepper
- ½ teaspoon dried thyme
- Salt
- 1½ cups heavy cream
- ¼ cup cornstarch
- ½ cup cold water
- ¼ cup diced scallion

Combine first 9 ingredients in a stockpot. Simmer over medium heat until potatoes are fork tender, about 15 to 20 minutes.

Season to taste with salt. Add cream. Return to a simmer. Combine cornstarch and cold water and add to soup. (The longer this soup sits, the thicker it will become. If soup becomes too thick, add more cream or stock.) Serve garnished with scallions.

Louisiana Sausage and Bean Soup

SERVES 8

When I was young, my mom would put out a pot of navy beans and a pan of corn bread. It wasn't a fancy meal, but it was a favorite. There's something about a hearty bean soup that still makes me feel warm and content.

½ pound dry navy beans
1 cup diced andouille sausage
1½ cups diced fresh tomatoes
½ cup medium diced celery
½ cup medium diced carrots
½ cup medium diced onions
1 teaspoon chopped fresh garlic
2 quarts chicken stock
1 teaspoon thyme
1 bay leaf
¼ teaspoon cayenne pepper
¼ teaspoon black pepper
2 tablespoons cornstarch
2 tablespoons cold water
Salt

Soak beans in cold water for several hours or overnight.

Sauté sausage in a large skillet or pot over medium-high heat for 5 to 10 minutes. Drain beans and add to skillet or pot. Add vegetables and garlic and sauté for 3 minutes. Stir in stock, thyme, bay leaf, and cayenne and black peppers. Bring to a boil. Reduce heat and simmer for 1 hour or until beans are tender.

Combine cornstarch and cold water in a small bowl. Return soup to a boil. Add cornstarch mixture to soup to thicken to your desired consistency. Season with salt to taste.

Roasted Red Pepper Tomato Bisque

SERVES 4

A neighbor of mine grows gorgeous Jersey tomatoes. Maybe too many tomatoes! She brings baskets of them to my family. To thank her, I came up with this recipe. For a perfect summer supper, add crawfish or crab and serve it with some good French or Italian bread.

2 tablespoons soy oil or olive oil
½ medium yellow onion, diced
½ stalk celery, diced
1 tablespoon garlic
½ cup chopped fresh basil
6 roasted red peppers
6 large red Jersey tomatoes, peeled, seeded, and diced
2 cups chicken stock or vegetable stock
Salt and pepper to taste
½ cup heavy cream

Heat oil in a 4-quart stockpot over medium-high heat. Add onion, celery, and garlic. Sauté until translucent.

Add basil, red peppers, tomatoes, and stock. Simmer for 15 minutes. Puree with hand blender or in food processor until smooth. Return to pot.

Season with salt and pepper. Add cream. Simmer until liquid is reduced and thick, about 10 minutes. Taste and adjust seasoning.

Smoked Tomato Crab Bisque

SERVES 4

This soup is a standard on the Melange Cafe menu. Rich and creamy with big lumps of crabmeat and smoky tomato slices, it's just about a meal in itself. In fact, Connie likes to serve it over pasta as an entree.

2 tablespoons butter
1 medium yellow onion, chopped
1 tomato, diced
½ stalk celery, roughly chopped
1 tablespoon chopped fresh garlic
3 tablespoons Old Bay Seasoning
2 bay leaves
3 cups whole milk
¼ cup Blond Roux (Recipe appears on page 116.)
½ cup heavy cream
¼ cup sherry
8 ounces jumbo lump crabmeat
Salt and white pepper to taste
4 slices smoked tomatoes, ½-inch thick each

Melt butter in a 4-quart stockpot over medium-high heat. Add onion, tomato, celery, garlic, Old Bay, and bay leaves. Sweat for 2 minutes. Add milk. Bring to a simmer and cook until vegetables are translucent, about 10 minutes. Strain. Discard solids and reserve liquid.

Heat roux over medium-high heat. Add hot milk. Simmer, stirring constantly, until thickened. Add cream, sherry, and crabmeat. Cook for about 2 minutes or until heated through. Taste and season with salt and pepper.

Place a tomato in each bowl. Ladle in soup and serve.

TO SMOKE TOMATOES: To smoke tomatoes, you will need two roasting pans, one rack, and hickory wood chips. Preheat oven to 400° or light your grill. Soak chips in water according to package instructions. Strain and place chips in the first roasting pan. Cover the rack with foil and place over chips. Invert the second roasting pan and cover rack. Place pans in oven or on grill. Let the hickory chips build up smoke. Remove inverted pan, place tomatoes on foil rack, and recover. Smoke for 15 minutes. Remove tomatoes and let cool. If this seems too complicated, call me or go to the store and purchase natural liquid smoke. Put one drop on each tomato and bake in a 350° oven for 10 minutes.

Lamb Stew with Lentils

SERVES 4 TO 6

Strong flavors from foods like lemon, garlic, tomatoes, and bay bring out the best in lamb.

3 pounds lamb, cut into cubes
Flour
2 tablespoons olive oil
2 cups chopped onion
2 cloves garlic, chopped
1 cup lentils
1 carrot, peeled and diced
1 cup crushed tomatoes
2 cups chicken stock
1 tablespoon minced lemon zest
Pinch of dried thyme
1 bay leaf

Dredge lamb in flour. Heat oil in a large stockpot over medium-high heat. Add lamb and brown on all sides.

Add onion and garlic and cook until transparent.

Add remaining ingredients and simmer until lentils and lamb are tender, about 1 hour or so.

Efo Fish Stew

SERVES 4

We serve this Nigerian dish as part of our Black History Month celebration. *Efo,* which means "greens" in Nigerian, is sort of the great-grandfather to green gumbo and similar to *callaloo*, a chile-spiked pot of greens cooked with salted and fresh fish from the Caribbean.

1 yellow onion, chopped
4 tomatoes, diced
2 cloves garlic, chopped
1 teaspoon dried thyme
½ teaspoon red pepper flakes
3 tablespoons red palm oil or vegetable oil
Salt
3 cups water
1½ pounds white fish fillets, cut into 1-inch pieces
1 pound spinach, stems removed and chopped
½ pound medium shrimp, peeled and deveined
Pepper

Combine onion, tomatoes, garlic, thyme, red pepper flakes, palm oil, salt, and water in a large pot. Bring to a boil over high heat. Continue boiling until liquid is reduced to 1 cup.

Add fish and cook until tender, about 5 minutes. Stir in spinach and cook for 10 minutes.

Add shrimp. Cover and cook until shrimp turn pink, about 3 to 4 minutes. Season to taste with salt and pepper.

Crawfish Gumbo

SERVES 4

My friend Bill Fisher is a big gumbo fan. When Bill decided to visit New Orleans, I told him to try a bunch of different gumbos. He took my advice and ate gumbo at every meal! (Even brunch!) His favorite? Mine. The man has good taste.

2 tablespoons soy oil
½ cup diced celery
½ cup medium diced onion
½ cup medium diced green pepper
2 cups sliced andouille sausage
1 cup chopped tomatoes, peeled and seeded
8 cups chicken or fish stock
1 tablespoon chopped fresh garlic
2 tablespoons Joe's Cajun Seasoning **(Recipe appears on page 117.)**
1 tablespoon dried thyme
½ teaspoon cayenne pepper
½ teaspoon black pepper
1 pound cooked and peeled crawfish meat
½ cup Dark Roux **(Recipe appears on page 116.)**
1 cup cooked long grain white rice, hot
Salt

Heat oil in a 12-quart stockpot over high heat. Add celery, onion, green pepper, and sausage. Cook until onion is translucent and sausage starts to render its fat.

Add tomatoes, stock, garlic, Joe's Cajun Seasoning, thyme, cayenne pepper, and black pepper and bring to a boil. Add crawfish and return to a boil. Reduce heat to medium and simmer about 20 minutes.

Add roux to thicken. (More roux may be added, if you prefer a thicker gumbo.)

Remove pot from heat. Add cooked rice and stir to combine well. Season to taste with salt. Serve hot in large bowls.

Lobster Gumbo

SERVES 4

Gumbo is basically a thick, hearty soup made with any variety of seafood, shellfish, sausage, ham, chicken, and vegetables. Gumbo is not a fussy food: filling and fabulous, yes; fussy, no. So the addition of lobster doesn't really make this dish gourmet; it's just "more good," as a young restaurant customer so correctly stated.

4 lobster tails
2 tablespoons soy oil
½ cup diced celery
½ cup medium diced onion
½ cup medium diced green pepper
1 cup peeled and seeded chopped tomatoes
8 cups fish stock
1 tablespoon chopped fresh garlic
2 tablespoons Joe's Cajun Seasoning (Recipe appears on page 117.)
1 tablespoon dried thyme
½ teaspoon cayenne pepper
½ teaspoon black pepper
½ cup Dark Roux (Recipe appears on page 116.)
1 cup cooked long grain white rice, hot
Salt

Partially split tails vertically. Pull meat partially away from shell, keeping tail end attached. Reserve.

Heat oil in a 12-quart stockpot over high heat. Add celery, onion, and green pepper. Cook until onion is translucent.

Add tomatoes, stock, garlic, Joe's Cajun Seasoning, thyme, cayenne pepper, and black pepper and bring to a boil. Add lobster and return to a boil. Reduce heat to medium and simmer about 20 minutes. Add roux to thicken. (More roux may be added, if you prefer a thicker gumbo.) Remove pot from heat. Add cooked rice and stir to combine well. Season to taste with salt. Serve hot in large bowls.

ONE POTS
AND PASTA

Seafood Jambalaya

SERVES 4 TO 6

I know you'll like our northern version of the classic southern tradition. What I like most about jambalaya is that there's no "right" way to make one. Some have tomatoes, some don't, and on and on. As the saying goes . . . there are as many versions of jambalaya and gumbo as there are Cajuns and Acadians in Louisiana.

8 tablespoons soy oil
1 cup sliced smoked andouille sausage
1 cup diced tasso ham
20 (20-30 count) sea scallops
8 (16-20 count) shrimp, peeled and deveined
8 whole crawfish, cleaned
1 cup diced green pepper
1 cup diced white onion
1 cup chopped scallions
20 mussels, cleaned and debearded
16 littleneck clams, cleaned and scrubbed
6 tablespoons chopped fresh garlic
8 teaspoons Joe's Cajun Seasoning
8 cups cooked white rice
4 cups chicken or seafood stock

Heat oil in large skillet over high heat. Add sausage and tasso ham. Sauté for 1 minute.

Add scallops, shrimp, crawfish, green pepper, white onion, and scallions. Sauté for 3 minutes. Add mussels, clams, garlic, and 6 teaspoons Joe's Cajun Seasoning. Sauté for 2 minutes.

Add rice and chicken stock. Cover and cook until liquid is reduced by three-quarters and clams are all open.

Serve in large bowls. Garnish with remaining Joe's Cajun Seasoning.

Vegetable Jambalaya

SERVES 4 TO 6

Before she was my publicist, Connie was a customer. She loves the one-pot meals – red beans and rice, gumbo, and especially, jambalaya. When she eliminated meat and fish from her diet, I made this dish for her. Now it's a popular dinner special for both vegetarians and meat eaters.

8 tablespoons soy oil
1 cup diced Japanese eggplant
1 cup sliced okra
2 corn cobs, quartered
1 cup sliced mixed wild mushrooms, stemmed
1 cup diced tomato
1 cup diced green pepper
1 cup diced white onion
1 cup chopped scallions
2 teaspoons fresh chopped garlic
8 teaspoons Joe's Cajun Seasoning **(Recipe appears on page 117.)**
8 cups cooked white rice
4 cups vegetable stock or water
1 cup roughly chopped firmly packed fresh spinach

Heat oil in large skillet over high heat. Add all vegetables, except spinach, and sauté for 1 minute. Add 6 teaspoons Joe's Cajun Seasoning. Sauté for 2 minutes. Add rice and vegetable stock.

Cover and cook until liquid is reduced by three-quarters and corn is done, about 20 to 25 minutes. Stir in spinach and cook for 2 minutes more.

Serve in large bowls and garnish with remaining Joe's Cajun Seasoning.

Breaux Bridge Crawfish Étouffée

SERVES 4

This recipe was inspired by Breaux Bridge in St. Martin's Parish where crawfish étouffée originated. Located on Bayou Teche, this small town is now the home of the world-famous crawfish festival.

¼ cup medium diced green pepper
¼ cup diced celery
¼ cup diced onions
1 cup diced tomatoes
1 cup cooked and peeled crawfish meat (Shrimp may be substituted.)
6 whole crawfish, cleaned (Shrimp may be substituted.)
2 cups chicken or seafood stock or water
1 teaspoon chopped fresh garlic
1 tablespoon Joe's Cajun Seasoning (Recipe appears on page 117.)
1 teaspoon thyme
2 tablespoons Dark Roux (Recipe appears on page 116.)

Combine veggies in a large skillet over medium-high heat. Sweat for 2 minutes. Chop crawfish and add to skillet. Add stock, garlic, Joe's Cajun Spice, and thyme. Bring to a boil.

Stir in dark roux and simmer until thick.

Serve immediately over steamed rice, pasta, or Crawfish Cakes (Recipe appears on page 96.).

Seafood Cioppino

SERVES 4

Cioppino is a classic stew created by San Francisco Italian immigrants. My version, a little bit more southern Louisiana than northern California, relies on a great variety of shellfish and squid, but you can substitute whatever fresh fish and shellfish you prefer and is available.

¼ cup olive oil
1 tablespoon fresh chopped garlic
1 pound fresh white fish (catfish, bass, rock cod), skinned and boned
1 pound squid, cut into strips
12 shrimp (16-20 size), peeled and deveined
12 large sea scallops
12 littleneck clams, scrubbed
12 mussels, cleaned and debearded
½ cup diced green pepper
½ cup diced scallions
½ cup sliced fennel
4 cups seafood stock
½ cup white wine
8 plum tomatoes, peeled and seeded or 1 can (28 ounces) plum tomatoes
1 tablespoon fresh oregano
1 tablespoon fresh basil
1 teaspoon red pepper flakes
Salt and pepper

Heat oil in a large stockpot over medium-high heat. Add garlic and sauté for 1 minute.

Cut fish into bite-size chunks. Add fish, squid, shellfish, and vegetables. Stir to combine and cook for 2 minutes.

Stir in stock, wine, tomatoes, oregano, basil, and red pepper flakes. Simmer for 5 minutes.

Bring to boil. Reduce heat to medium and cook until clams and mussels are open. Season to taste with salt and pepper.

Serve immediately in soup bowls with good bread for sopping or over your favorite pasta.

NOTE: If fresh spices are not available, dried may be substituted. Use 1½ teaspoons dried instead of 1 tablespoon fresh.

Chicken, Red Beans, and Rice

SERVES 4

In days past, Monday was wash day in Louisiana. Since the chore took all day, a pot of red beans would be set out to simmer. When the washing was done, the beans were ready. My recipe strays a bit from the traditional with the inclusion of brown sugar and peaches, but I think those wash day women of yesteryear would approve.

4 skinless, boneless chicken breasts (about 6 ounces each), pounded
Pinch each of salt and pepper
Flour
4 tablespoons vegetable oil
¼ cup sliced andouille sausage
¼ cup medium diced green pepper
½ cup diced scallions
1 cup canned dark red kidney beans
1 teaspoon chopped fresh garlic
1 tablespoon Joe's Cajun Seasoning **(Recipe appears on page 117.)**
1 tablespoon brown sugar
1 teaspoon dried thyme
1½ cups chicken stock
4 cups cooked white rice
1 peach, sliced or ½ cup canned sliced cling peaches in syrup
3 tablespoons sour cream, optional
France's Cheese Biscuits **(Recipe appears on page 114.)****, optional**

Season each breast with a pinch each of salt and pepper. Lightly flour.

Heat oil in a large sauté pan over medium-high heat. Add chicken and sauté for about 2 minutes per side. Add sausage, green pepper, and scallions. Sauté for 2 minutes. Add beans, garlic, Joe's Cajun Seasoning, brown sugar, and thyme. Stir until well combined.

Add stock, rice, and peaches. Simmer until stock is fully absorbed, about 10 minutes. Serve chicken over rice and garnish with sour cream. Serve alone or with France's Cheese Biscuits.

Louisiana Dirty Rice and Clams

SERVES 4

Sautéed chicken livers make this classic Louisiana dish a little "dirty" and a lot tasty.

- **3 tablespoons soy oil**
- **½ cup chopped fresh chicken livers**
- **½ cup sliced andouille sausage**
- **½ cup chopped green pepper**
- **½ cup diced onion**
- **24 littleneck clams, scrubbed**
- **4 cups cooked long grain white rice**
- **4 cups chicken stock**
- **2 tablespoons Joe's Cajun Seasoning (Recipe appears on page 117.)**
- **1 tablespoon chopped fresh garlic**

Heat oil over medium-high heat. Add chicken livers, sausage, green pepper, and onion. Sauté about 10 minutes or until chicken livers are good and dirty, meaning brown with bits and pieces stuck on the bottom of the pan.

Add clams, rice, chicken stock, Joe's Cajun Seasoning, and garlic. Simmer until all moisture is absorbed and clams are open, about 5 to 10 minutes.

Serve in a large casserole bowl with rice on the bottom and clams piled on top.

Risotto with Wild Mushrooms and Chicken Livers

SERVES 4

Some people don't make risotto because they think it takes a lot of time. I'm not going to lie to you: it does take a while, but I think the result is worth the effort. You'll notice that the directions call for you to stir constantly. That is not a typo. Stirring creates friction which softens the outer hull of the rice. This is what makes it creamy, melt-in-you-mouth risotto and not just flavored rice.

8 tablespoons butter
1 cup finely chopped onion
2 cloves garlic, minced
1 cup Arborio rice
⅔ cup white wine
2 cups chicken stock
4 ounces fresh wild mushrooms, sliced
1 pound chicken livers, trimmed and quartered
1 tablespoon lemon juice
Salt and pepper to taste
¼ cup chopped parsley
⅓ cup grated Parmesan cheese

Heat 4 tablespoons butter in a heavy skillet or saucepan over moderate heat until foaming. Add onion and garlic and sauté until golden brown, about 10 minutes.

Add rice, stir well, and cook for about 2 minutes. Add wine and stir until it has been absorbed. Add stock, ½ cup at a time, stirring constantly. Allow each portion of stock to be fully absorbed before adding the next. After first cup of stock has been absorbed, add mushrooms.

Meanwhile, sauté chicken livers in a separate pan in remaining butter until just browned. Stir in lemon juice.

When all stock has been absorbed, season risotto to taste with salt and pepper and add livers, parsley, and cheese.

NOTE: Two ounces dried wild mushrooms soaked in ¼ cup warm water can be substituted for fresh.

Penne Alla Arrabiata

SERVES 4

How could this dish go wrong with all these great Italian ingredients?

- 2 tablespoons extra virgin olive oil
- 8 ounces hot Italian sausage, cut into ¼-inch-thick rounds
- 2 cups medium diced tomatoes
- 2 cups firmly packed fresh spinach
- 1 cup sliced mushrooms
- 1 teaspoon chopped fresh garlic
- ½ cup white wine
- 1 tablespoon chopped fresh basil
- 1 teaspoon red pepper flakes
- 2 cups chicken stock
- 1 tablespoon tomato paste
- 1 pound penne pasta or tricolored cheese tortellini, cooked
- 4 tablespoons cold butter
- Salt and pepper
- 4 sprigs basil

Heat oil in a large skillet or pot over medium-high heat. Add sausage and brown for about 2 minutes. Drain oil.

Add tomatoes, spinach, mushrooms, garlic, and white wine and cook for about 2 minutes. Stir in chopped basil and red pepper flakes. Add stock and bring to a boil. Stir in tomato paste.

Add cooked pasta. Whisk in butter, a little at a time. Season with salt and pepper to taste.

Serve family style garnished with basil sprigs.

Crawfish Pasta in Tasso Cajun Cream

SERVES 4

I especially like this dish because it combines two of my favorite Louisiana specialties – crawfish and tasso. Not only are crawfish great as a meal all by themselves, but they are useful in making a variety of sauces. Tasso is highly seasoned Cajun cured pork – the New Orleans version of pancetta or proscuitto but much more robust. Red peppers, garlic, and filé powder give it that strong, spicy flavor.

½ pound uncooked penne pasta
4 tablespoons butter
¼ pound tasso ham, finely chopped
1 cup thinly sliced green onions
2 teaspoons minced garlic
2 cups heavy cream
1 teaspoon salt
1 teaspoon pepper
½ teaspoon Joe's Cajun Seasoning (Recipe appears on page 117.)
½ pound crawfish tails, peeled

Cook pasta according to package directions. Do not over-cook. Rinse in cold water and set aside.

Melt butter in a large skillet. Add tasso and sauté until lightly browned. Add green onions and garlic. Stir for about 1 minute. Stir in cream, salt, pepper, and Joe's Cajun Seasoning . Bring to a boil and cook for about 2 minutes until slightly thickened.

Add crawfish tails, return to a boil, and cook for 1 minute. Mix in pasta and cook until pasta is heated through. Serve immediately.

Garlic Shrimp and Pasta

SERVES 4

Garlic, shrimp, olive oil, and basil are magic ingredients. A quick sauté with a splash of white wine to bind the flavors together and you have a most delicious meal in about 15 minutes.

- **1 pound capellini (angel hair) pasta, fresh or dried**
- **¼ cup extra virgin olive oil**
- **24 large shrimp, peeled and deveined**
- **½ cup chopped scallions**
- **2 tablespoons chopped fresh garlic**
- **2 tablespoons chopped fresh basil**
- **2 tablespoons Joe's Cajun Seasoning (Recipe appears on page 117.)**
- **¼ cup white wine**
- **3 cups fish or chicken stock**
- **4 tablespoons cold butter, cubed**

Cook pasta according to package directions until al dente (or till it sticks on the wall). Strain and reserve.

Meanwhile, heat oil in a large skillet over medium-high heat. Add shrimp and sauté for 2 minutes per side. Add scallions, garlic, basil, and Joe's Cajun Seasoning. Stir to combine. Splash with wine and cook about 2 minutes. Add stock and cook until liquid is reduced by half.

Whisk butter into skillet until sauce is thickened and glossy. Serve immediately over hot pasta.

PLATED ENTREES

Smothered Chicken
with Crawfish Mashed Potatoes

SERVES 4

An old-fashioned way to cook chicken and gravy, this is my sister-in-law Kim's favorite chicken dish. Ask her about it, and she'll say it's "so good that Joe must have put his foot in it." (That's Southern slang for something that is so delicious, the cook must have put a part of himself in it.)

½ cup flour
1 teaspoon salt
½ teaspoon pepper
4 skinless chicken breasts (6 to 8 ounces each), pounded
½ cup vegetable oil
2 cups sliced onions
2 cups sliced domestic mushrooms
4 tablespoons chopped fresh garlic
2 tablespoons Joe's Cajun Seasoning (Recipe appears on page 117.)
3 cups chicken stock
4 tablespoons Dark Roux (Recipe appears on page 116.)
Crawfish Mashed Potatoes (see recipe)

Season flour with salt and pepper. Lightly coat chicken with flour. Heat oil in a large sauté pan over high heat. Add chicken and sauté for 2 minutes on each side.

Add onions and mushrooms and sauté for 2 minutes. Stir in garlic and Joe's Cajun Seasoning. Add chicken stock and bring to a simmer. Add dark roux. Continue to simmer until thickened.

Place mashed potatoes on a plate or in a bowl. Cover with chicken and smother with onion and mushroom gravy.

Crawfish Mashed Potatoes

SERVES 4

5 to 6 red bliss potatoes, halved
¾ cup milk
¼ cup butter
2 tablespoons chopped fresh garlic
Salt and pepper
1 cup cooked crawfish meat (Lobster, crab, or shrimp can be substituted.)

Cook potatoes in boiling water until fork-tender, about 12 to 15 minutes. Strain and reserve.

Combine milk, butter, garlic, and salt and pepper to taste in a saucepan. Bring to a simmer over medium heat. Place potatoes in a food processor or mash by hand. Gradually add hot milk mixture. Pulse or mash until well combined. Fold in crawfish. Season with salt and pepper.

Southern Fried Chicken

SERVES 4

Southern fried chicken is probably the most all-American chicken recipe. I know I feel downright patriotic when I eat it! Soaking the chicken and shaking well results in amazing crispness and flavor. Serve chicken with collard greens for a true Southern experience.

1 whole chicken (3 to 4 pounds), cut into serving pieces or 3 to 4 pounds chicken parts
1½ cups ice water
1 cup all-purpose flour
1 teaspoon paprika
1 teaspoon salt
½ teaspoon sugar
½ teaspoon garlic powder
½ teaspoon black pepper
¼ teaspoon cayenne pepper
2½ cups soy oil

Soak chicken pieces in ice water for 15 minutes to seal in juices.

Combine flour, paprika, salt, sugar, garlic powder, black pepper, and cayenne pepper in a brown paper bag. One by one, remove chicken from ice water and drop into bag. Close and shake until chicken is well coated. Place coated chicken pieces on a baking sheet and refrigerate for 15 minutes.

Heat soy oil in a deep fryer or a deep heavy pan to 350°. (To test, dip a corner of chicken in the hot oil; if it immediately sizzles, it's ready.) Fry chicken, a few pieces at a time, until golden and cooked through, about 15 minutes. Drain on paper towels. Serve hot or cold.

Collard Greens

SERVES 4

The most important thing I can tell you about collard greens is that they take time. If you have the time to give, you will be rewarded with a wonderful side dish filled with a great smoky flavor and plenty of iron. Just remember . . . time is the beginning of all great things to come.

1 pound ham hocks or smoked turkey, cut into 2-inch pieces
5 quarts water
1 tablespoon red pepper flakes
1 large bunch collard greens (about 2 to 2½ pounds), washed well and roughly cut
3 tablespoons white vinegar
Salt

Combine ham or turkey, water, and red pepper flakes in a large heavy pot. Bring to a boil. Reduce heat and simmer for 30 minutes. Add collards and vinegar and cook until very tender, about 30 to 40 minutes. Season to taste with salt.

Cajun Turkey
with Dirty Rice Stuffing

SERVES 12

This recipe appeared in *Cooking Light* magazine. Yeah, I know, most of my recipes are on the "heavy" side of light, but I was happy to create this recipe and proud to be included in such a wonderful publication.

1 fresh or thawed frozen turkey (12 pounds)
2 tablespoons Joe's Cajun Seasoning (Recipe appears on page 117.)
½ teaspoon salt
½ teaspoon pepper
Butter
Dirty Rice Stuffing (see recipe)

Preheat oven to 350°. Remove neck and giblets from turkey and discard. Rinse turkey with cold water and pat dry. Trim excess fat. Starting at neck cavity, loosen skin from breast and drumsticks by inserting finger and gently pushing between skin and meat. Rub Joe's Cajun Seasoning, salt, and pepper onto meat under loosened skin. Tie ends of legs with cord or string.

Place turkey on a broiler pan or on a rack set in a shallow roasting pan. Rub turkey skin with butter and season with additional salt and pepper, if desired. Insert meat thermometer into meaty part of thigh, making sure it does not touch the bone. Roast for 2 ½ hours or until thermometer reaches 180°.

Remove turkey from oven. Cover loosely with foil and let stand 10 minutes before carving. Serve with stuffing.

Dirty Rice Stuffing

SERVES 12

2 tablespoons soy oil
1 pound andouille sausage, chopped
½ pound chicken livers, cut into bite-size pieces
1 cup finely chopped onion
1 cup finely chopped celery
1 cup finely chopped green pepper
¼ cup Joe's Cajun Seasoning **(Recipe appears on page 117.)**
¼ cup chopped fresh garlic
6 cups cooked long-grain rice
3 cups chicken stock
½ teaspoon salt

Heat oil in a stockpot or deep skillet over medium-high heat.

Add sausage, livers, onion, celery, pepper, Joe's Cajun Seasoning, and garlic. Sauté for 15 minutes or until brown.

Add rice, stock, and salt. Cook until liquid is absorbed, about 15 minutes.

Grilled Rib-eye with Rosemary Jus

with Garlic Mashed Potatoes and Caramelized Mushrooms and Onions

SERVES 4

Eric Duber has been cooking with me since Melange Cafe opened. He has a love/hate relationship with this very popular recipe. He loves, loves, *loves* to eat the garlic mashed potatoes but hates to make them. And like we said . . . it's a very popular dish.

- **4 rib-eye steaks (10 ounces each)**
- **4 teaspoons Joe's Cajun Seasoning (Recipe appears on page 117.)**
- **4 cups soy oil**
- **¼ cup Worcestershire sauce**
- **¼ cup A.1. Steak Sauce**
- **1 tablespoon chopped fresh garlic**
- **1 cup beef stock**
- **1 cup burgundy red wine**
- **2 tablespoons fresh rosemary or 1 tablespoon dried**
- **Salt to taste**
- **Garlic Mashed Potatoes (see recipe)**
- **Caramelized Mushrooms and Onions (see recipe)**

Season steaks with Joe's Cajun Seasoning. Combine soy oil, Worcestershire, A.1., and garlic in a shallow glass or ceramic bowl or pan. Add steaks, cover, and marinate in refrigerator for 1 to 6 hours.

Heat grill to medium-high. Remove steaks from marinade and grill about 10 minutes per side or until desired doneness.

Meanwhile, simmer beef stock, wine, and rosemary over medium-high heat until liquid is reduced by half. Season with salt to taste. Reserve.

Place garlic mashed potatoes in centers of serving plates. Top with steak and caramelized mushrooms and onions. Nap with rosemary jus.

Garlic Mashed Potatoes

SERVES 4

5 to 6 red bliss potatoes, halved
¾ cup milk
¼ cup butter
2 tablespoons chopped fresh garlic
Salt and pepper

Cook potatoes in boiling water until fork-tender, about 12 to 15 minutes. Strain. Place potatoes in a food processor or mash by hand.

Combine milk, butter, and garlic in a saucepan. Bring to a simmer over medium heat.

Gradually add hot milk mixture to potatoes. Pulse or mash until well combined. Season to taste with salt and pepper.

Caramelized Mushrooms and Onions

SERVES 4

2 tablespoons soy oil
1 cup sliced fresh mushrooms
2 cups sliced white onions
¼ cup sugar
1 tablespoon Joe's Cajun Seasoning
(Recipe appears on page 117.)

Heat oil in skillet over medium-high heat. Add mushrooms and onions and sauté until just transparent. Stir in sugar and Joe's Cajun Seasoning.

Reduce heat to medium. Cook, stirring occasionally, until mixture is golden and sticky.

Steak Diane

SERVES 4

Steak Diane isn't hip or trendy or cool. It's just easy to prepare (all in one pan) and delicious to eat. Simple as that.

4 strip loin steaks
3 cloves garlic, crushed
Freshly ground black pepper
4 tablespoons butter
4 scallions, finely chopped
2 teaspoons Dijon mustard
2 tablespoons Worcestershire sauce
1 tablespoon brandy
½ cup cream
2 tablespoons chopped parsley

Place steaks between two sheets of wax paper or plastic wrap and pound to ¼-inch thick. Unwrap and spread each side with garlic and a grind of fresh pepper.

Heat 2 tablespoons butter in a large sauté pan over medium-high heat. When butter is melted, raise heat to high and cook steaks for 1 minute on each side. Lower heat to medium-high and cook 1 to 4 minutes on each side until desired doneness. Remove from pan and keep warm.

Melt remaining butter in same pan. Add scallions and cook 1 minute. Add mustard, Worcestershire sauce, and brandy. Stir to dislodge bits of meat from bottom of pan.

Stir in cream. Bring to a boil, then reduce heat and let simmer for about 3 minutes. Stir in parsley. Return steaks to pan and coat with sauce. Serve alone topped with sauce or with Garlic Mashed Potatoes (Recipe appears on page 79.).

Carpetbagger's Steak

SERVES 4

Versions of this recipe have been around for a long time. As a matter of fact, it appeared in the 1925 *California Cook Book*. Sometimes called Carpetbegger's Steak or Spanish Steak, I just call it good.

3 tablespoons butter
1 cup drained and chopped fresh oysters
½ cup chopped fresh mushrooms
2 teaspoons chopped fresh parsley
4 slices bacon, cooked and crumbled
1 ounce blue cheese, crumbled
¼ cup dry white wine
4 rib-eye steaks or steak fillets

Heat butter in a large sauté pan over medium-high heat. Add oysters, mushrooms, and parsley and sauté until mushrooms are tender. Drain off butter.

Stir in bacon, cheese, and wine and cook for about 5 minutes.

Preheat broiler. Cut a pocket into each steak. Stuff steaks with equal portions of oyster mixture, reserving about 4 tablespoons for garnish.

Broil steaks about 6 inches from heat for 8 to 10 minutes per side or until desired doneness. Top with reserved oyster mixture.

Veal Franchaise with Crabmeat

SERVES 4

The keys to this dish are a hot pan and a cool touch. Lightly coating the veal with flour prevents it from toughening and gives a crisp edge. Gently handling the crabmeat keeps the lumps intact and the flavor intense.

- 12 veal medallions (2 to 3 ounces each), pounded
- Salt and pepper
- 1 cup flour
- 3 eggs
- 2 cups soy oil
- Juice of 1 lemon
- ¼ cup white wine
- 1 cup chicken stock
- ½ cup grated Parmesan cheese
- ¼ cup unsalted butter, cubed
- 1 pound fresh jumbo lump crabmeat, picked clean

Lightly season medallions on each side with salt and pepper. Dredge in flour, tapping off excess. Beat eggs. Dip veal into eggs.

Heat oil in large skillet over medium-high heat. Gently place medallions in hot oil. Brown on each side for 2 minutes each or until golden brown. Remove from oil and drain on paper towel. Discard oil.

Return veal to pan but remove from heat. Add fresh lemon juice and wine. Stir to remove bits from bottom of pan. Pour in stock. Return pan to heat. Bring to a simmer over medium-high heat.

Transfer medallions to serving plates.

Add Parmesan cheese to sauce. Whisk in butter, a little at a time. Simmer for 1 minute. Add crabmeat and cook 2 minutes. Top veal medallions with crabmeat and sauce.

Tasso-Stuffed Pork Chops

SERVES 6

In Steven Raichlen's great book *How to Grill,* he says, "If ever there was a cut of meat ripe for stuffing, it's the pork chop. A stuffing – even a simple one – does much to dignify this simple, straightforward cut." Not surprisingly I agree and hope you enjoy this simple stuffed chop.

5 tablespoons olive oil
2 slices bread, cut into 1-inch cubes
½ cup finely chopped onions
½ cup finely chopped celery
2 tablespoons finely chopped tasso
¼ cup beef stock
½ teaspoon Joe's Cajun Seasoning (Recipe appears on page 117.)
Salt and pepper to taste
6 center-cut pork chops, about 1½ inches thick
1 large egg, beaten
Breadcrumbs

Heat 2 tablespoons oil in a sauté pan over medium-high heat. Add bread cubes and pan fry until crispy. Remove from pan and drain on paper towels. Reserve in a bowl.

Heat remaining oil in same pan. Add onions, celery, and tasso and sauté for about 5 minutes or until soft. Add stock and Joe's Cajun Seasoning. Season to taste with salt and pepper. Pour over bread cubes and toss to mix.

Preheat oven to 350°. Cut a pocket into each chop. Stuff chops with equal portions of bread mixture. Dip chops in egg and then dredge in breadcrumbs. Place in lightly oiled shallow baking pan. Cover lightly with foil. Bake for 1 hour and 30 minutes or until cooked through.

Citrus Chilean Sea Bass

SERVES 4

You will love this brightly flavored entree, IF you take my advice. Make the sauce first, remove it from the heat, and reserve; otherwise, the sauce will break and spoil your sunny supper. I created this sauce while working at Landmark Inn. It's light and fruity and a perfect complement to any white fish, salmon, shrimp, or chicken.

- 4 Chilean sea bass fillets (6 to 7 ounces each), skins on
- 2 tablespoons lemon pepper
- 4 tablespoons soy oil
- Juice of 1 lemon
- 3 ounces orange juice
- 3 ounces grapefruit juice
- 2 tablespoons heavy cream
- ¼ cup sliced yellow onion
- 1 small bay leaf
- ¼ pound unsalted butter, cut into cubes
- 1 head bok choy
- Sweet Potato Fries or Sliced Fried Potatoes (see recipes)

Preheat oven to 350°. Season sea bass with lemon pepper. Heat large ovenproof skillet over high heat. Add 2 tablespoons oil. Slowly add fillets and sear for 1 minute on each side.

Transfer to oven and bake until cooked through and flaky, about 8 to 10 minutes, depending on thickness.

Meanwhile, combine fruit juices, cream, onion, and bay leaf in a medium saucepan. Heat over medium-high heat until liquid is reduced by three-quarters.

Gradually add butter to sauce, stirring constantly, until all butter is combined. Remove from heat. Remove bay leaf. Reserve until ready to serve.

Heat remaining oil in a sauté pan over medium-high heat. Roughly chop bok choy (both white and green parts). Add to pan and stir fry for 2 to 3 minutes. Remove from heat.

Arrange bok choy in centers of plates and top with fish. Drizzle on sauce. Serve with sweet potato fries or sliced fried potatoes.

Sweet Potato Fries

SERVES 4

Don't save sweet potatoes just for special occassions. I like them all year long — baked, mashed, roasted, or fried. Look for firm dark sweets with no bruises or knobs.

2 sweet potatoes
Soy oil
Salt and freshly ground black pepper

Peel sweet potatoes and cut into long, flat planks.

Heat oil to 350° in a large skillet over medium-high heat. Add potatoes and fry until golden brown and cooked through, about 4 minutes.

Remove from oil with tongs or slotted spoon. Drain on paper towel. Season with salt and pepper to taste. Keep hot in warm oven until ready to serve.

Sliced Fried Potatoes

SERVES 4

4 cups soy oil
2 large Idaho or russet potatoes, sliced into ¼-inch rounds
Salt and pepper
Joe's Cajun Seasoning (Recipe appears on page 117.)

Heat oil to 350° in a large skillet over medium-high heat. Add potatoes and fry until golden brown and cooked through, about 4 minutes.

Drain on paper towel. Season with salt and pepper and Joe's Cajun Seasoning to taste.

Country Fried Catfish

with Corn Mock-Shoo

SERVES 4

In the South, it's typical to serve fried fish for supper on Fridays and for breakfast on Sundays. Whether it's a.m. or p.m., you'll love how simple this all-in-one meal is to make and how good it tastes.

4 catfish fillets (4 to 6 ounces each)
2 tablespoons Joe's Cajun Seasoning **(Recipe appears on page 117.)**
2 cups corn meal
1 cup flour
1 tablespoon salt
3 cups soy oil
Corn Mock-Shoo (see recipe)

Lightly season fillets on each side with 1 tablespoon seasoning. Combine remaining seasoning, corn meal, flour, and salt in a paper bag. Place fillets in bag and shake it like your mamma told you until fish are well coated. Reserve.

Heat oil to 350° in large skillet over medium-high heat.

Gently add fish to skillet and fry for 4 to 5 minutes per side, depending on thickness, until golden brown and cooked through. Drain on paper towel. Serve topped with corn mock-shoo.

Corn Mock-Shoo

SERVES 4

In New Orleans they call this dish *maque choux.* But I'm cooking in New Jersey, and we say mock-shoo. Yo! You got a problem with that?

2 tablespoons soy oil
1 cup cooked corn kernels
¼ cup diced yellow onion
¼ cup diced green pepper
¼ cup diced scallions
¼ cup diced fresh tomato
½ cup heavy cream
1 teaspoon Joe's Cajun Seasoning (Recipe appears on page 117.)
Salt and pepper

Heat oil in a large skillet over medium heat. Add corn, onion, green pepper, and scallions. Sauté until onions are transparent. Stir in tomato and cream. Cook until liquid is reduced by half. Season with Joe's Cajun Seasoning and salt and pepper to taste. Serve as a side or on top of catfish.

Seared Catfish with Crawfish Ratatouille

SERVES 4

This recipe unites eggplant and zucchini with traditional "N'Awlins" flavors, resulting in a delicious marriage between the Mediterranean Sea and the Mississippi River.

2 catfish fillets (4 to 6 ounces each)
Salt and pepper
1 tablespoon olive oil
1 small onion, diced
1 green pepper, diced
1 medium eggplant, peeled and diced
1 medium zucchini, diced
1 medium yellow squash, diced
1 stalk celery, diced
1 teaspoon minced fresh garlic
1 tablespoon chopped fresh basil
1 tablespoon dried oregano
1 teaspoon salt
1 teaspoon freshly ground black pepper
2 medium tomatoes, peeled and chopped
1 pound cooked crawfish, peeled and chopped

Season catfish fillets with salt and pepper to taste. Heat a medium skillet over medium-high heat. Gently add fillets to skillet and cook for 4 to 5 minutes per side, depending on thickness, until cooked through. Reserve and keep warm.

Heat olive oil in a large skillet over medium-high heat. Add onion and green pepper and sauté until onion is translucent.

Add eggplant, zucchini, squash, and celery. Mix in garlic, basil, oregano, salt, and pepper and stir to combine. Add tomatoes. Reduce heat to low. Cover and cook for 10 minutes.

Add crawfish to vegetable mixture and simmer for 2 minutes. Place ratatouille on serving plates. Top with catfish.

Pan Crusted Salmon

over Wilted Spinach with Honey Balsamic Reduction

SERVES 4

Balsamic vinegar adds a jolt of spirit to marinades, dressings, and sauces. Fat free and full of flavor, it is a great accompaniment to fish, meat, vegetables, and even fruit, such as strawberries.

1 teaspoon granulated garlic
1 teaspoon black pepper
1 teaspoon dried thyme
1 teaspoon salt
4 salmon fillets (6 to 8 ounces each), skins on
6 tablespoons soy oil
4 cups firmly packed fresh spinach
2 cups sliced mushrooms
Salt and pepper
Honey Balsamic Reduction (see recipe)

Combine dried seasonings. Lightly dust salmon on each side with mixture. Reserve.

Preheat oven to 450°. Heat large skillet over high heat. Add 4 tablespoons oil to hot skillet. Gently lay fillets, skin sides down, in oil. Cook for 1 minute on each side. Remove from pan and transfer to baking sheet. Bake until desired doneness, about 4 to 6 minutes.

Meanwhile, heat remaining oil in skillet over medium-high heat. Add spinach and mushrooms. Season to taste with salt and pepper. Sauté gently for 2 to 3 minutes or until spinach is just wilted. Remove from heat.

Arrange vegetables in centers of plates. Top with fish. Drizzle with reduction.

Honey Balsamic Reduction

2 cups balsamic vinegar
¼ cup honey
1 tablespoon cornstarch
2 tablespoons cold water

Combine vinegar and honey in a heavy-bottomed saucepan. Bring to a boil over medium-high heat. Reduce heat to medium and cook until liquid is reduced by half. Mix cornstarch and water. Add to sauce and stir until thick.

Crawfish Potpie

SERVES 4

These pies freeze very well, so double the recipe and keep some in the freezer for a rainy day dinner. Allow to thaw overnight in the refrigerator prior to baking.

Short Pastry Crust (see recipe)
4 tablespoons butter
1 medium onion, finely chopped
3 tablespoons flour
1 cup heavy cream
2 tablespoons tomato paste
2 tablespoons brandy
2 tablespoons white wine
¼ teaspoon cayenne pepper
¼ teaspoon nutmeg
1 pound peeled crawfish tails
Salt and white pepper to taste
¼ cup milk

Divide dough in half and roll into two balls. Reserve one ball.

Divide other ball into quarters. Form each quarter into a ball and roll out on a lightly floured work surface. Fit each into an individual casserole dish. Divide reserve ball into quarters. Form each quarter into a ball and roll out to form "tops" for the dishes. Cover and refrigerate.

Melt butter in a saucepan over medium heat. Add onions and cook until transparent, being careful not to burn them. Add flour and stir to coat onions. Add cream and stir until thickened. Add paste, brandy, wine, cayenne, and nutmeg and mix well. Add crawfish tails and heat through. Season with salt and white pepper.

Remove mixture from heat and cool. Ladle cooled crawfish mixture into pie shells. Place tops over mixture and crimp edges to seal. Brush pastry with milk. Cut two steam vents into each pie. Refrigerate at least 30 minutes.

Preheat oven to 375°. Bake potpies until crusts are golden, about 35 or 40 minutes.

Short Pastry Crust

YIELDS 1 9-INCH DOUBLE PIE CRUST OR 4 MINI PIES

Short pastry crusts are crumbly and very rich. They're perfect for savory, creamy dishes such as these potpies or for sweet desserts like fruit tarts, dumplings, or galettes.

1⅔ cups flour
½ teaspoon salt
½ cup unsalted butter
1 egg, beaten lightly
2 to 4 teaspoons water

Sift together flour and salt. Use a pastry cutter or 2 knives to cut butter into flour until lumps are pea size. Add egg to mixture. Add water, 1 teaspoon at a time, mixing with a fork until flour is just moist and dough holds together.

Knead until combined but not overworked. Shape into a ball and chill for 30 minutes. Bake as directed in recipe.

Crab Cakes with Tomato-Basil Concassé

SERVES 4

Just about every chef has a "signature" crab cake recipe. I don't claim full ownership of this one, since it was influenced by the many chefs with whom I've worked over the years. I thank them all, and so will you.

1½ pounds lump crabmeat, picked clean
4 tablespoons breadcrumbs
¼ cup chopped fresh parsley
½ cup mayonnaise
2 tablespoons Worcestershire sauce
1 tablespoon Old Bay Seasoning
1 tablespoon Dijon mustard
2 cups flour
1 cup yellow corn meal
3 cups soy oil
Tomato-Basil Concassé (see recipe)

Combine crabmeat, breadcrumbs, parsley, mayonnaise, Worcestershire, Old Bay, and mustard. Form into eight 3-ounces patties.

Combine flour and corn meal. Lightly dust cakes with flour mixture and set aside.

Heat oil to 350° in a large skillet over medium-high heat. Add cakes and sauté for approximately 2 minutes on each side or until golden brown.

Drain on paper towel. Serve with tomato-basil concassé.

Tomato-Basil Concassé

2 tablespoons olive oil
1 tablespoon chopped garlic
2 tablespoons chopped fresh basil
2 cups diced fresh plum tomatoes
Salt and pepper to taste

Heat olive oil in a medium skillet over medium heat. Add garlic and basil. Cook for 15 seconds. Add tomatoes and salt and pepper to taste. Stir gently for 2 minutes. Taste and adjust seasoning.

Crawfish Cakes

SERVES 4

Crawfish are one of the staples of the Cajun diet and are considered a delicacy in many places outside of Louisiana. They are one of the tastiest, healthiest, and cheapest forms of seafood you can get.

2 cups cooked and peeled crawfish meat
½ cup chopped green pepper
½ cup chopped onion
¾ cup mayonnaise
2 tablespoons Worcestershire sauce
2 tablespoons Old Bay Seasoning
1 tablespoon Joe's Cajun Seasoning (Recipe appears on page 117.)
1 teaspoon chopped fresh garlic
Flour
3 eggs
1 cup milk
2 cups fresh or dried breadcrumbs
1 cup soy oil

Combine crawfish, green pepper, and onion in a food processor and pulse until chopped into a small but not fine dice. Transfer to mixing bowl. Stir in mayonnaise, Worcestershire, Old Bay, Joe's Cajun Spice, and garlic.

Form into 8 patties, about 3 ounces each.

Dredge cakes in flour and tap off excess. Combine eggs and milk in a small bowl. Brush cakes with egg wash. Dredge in breadcrumbs. Reserve in refrigerator until ready to cook.

Heat oil to 350° in a large skillet over medium heat. Add cakes and fry about 2 minutes per side or until brown. Drain on paper towel.

Serve cakes immediately . . . "naked" or with Breaux Bridge Crawfish Étouffée (Recipe appears on page 62.).

NOTE: Cakes can be made in advance. Just hold in a 300° oven.

DESSERTS

But I Want Chocolate Cake

SERVES 6

Several years ago, I was out in the dining room talking with customers when this cute 10-year-old said she liked everything on the menu but didn't understand why there was no chocolate cake for dessert. I told her we just didn't make it, and she let out a loud whine – "But I waannnttt it." Well, I listen to my customers, and this cake has become a favorite of mine (and my young protester).

4 tablespoons butter
2 ounces unsweetened chocolate
1 cup flour, sifted
1 pinch salt
¾ teaspoon baking soda
1 egg
1 cup sugar
¾ cup plus 2 tablespoons milk
1 teaspoon vanilla

Preheat oven to 350°. Butter and flour an 8-inch round cake pan. Reserve.

Melt butter and chocolate over medium heat until smooth. Reserve.

Mix flour, salt, and baking soda in a bowl. Reserve.

Combine egg and sugar in a large mixing bowl. Beat until thick and pale. Stir in melted chocolate. Fold in half of flour mixture; then half of milk. Repeat. Stir in vanilla.

Pour into prepared pan. Bake for 35 minutes or until surface is slightly springy to the touch. Serve warm or cooled.

Chocolate Grand Marnier Cheesecake

SERVES 8 TO 10

With its boozy orange flavor and bittersweet glaze, this is a grown-up cheesecake. Serve it whenever you want to make a seriously spectacular impression.

1 tablespoon cold butter
½ cup graham cracker crumbs
2 pounds cream cheese, softened
4 eggs
1¾ cups sugar
Grated rind and juice of 1 lemon
1 teaspoon vanilla
½ cup Grand Marnier
Chocolate Glaze (see recipe)

Heat oven to 325°. Butter the sides of an 8-inch-round x 3-inch-deep springform pan. Sprinkle sides with graham cracker crumbs and tap off excess.

Combine cream cheese, eggs, sugar, lemon rind and juice, and vanilla in a mixer or food processor. Beat or process until smooth. Pour into prepared pan. Place pan in a water bath. Bake for 1½ hours.

Turn oven off but leave cheesecake in oven for 30 minutes. Remove cheesecake from oven and water bath. Cool to room temperature. Unmold and refrigerate for 1 hour.

With a toothpick, poke holes all over top of cheesecake. Pour on Grand Marnier to fill holes and saturate cheese-cake. Let set for about 30 minutes. Pour chocolate glaze over cheesecake and refrigerate until chocolate hardens.

Chocolate Glaze

1 pound bittersweet chocolate
1 cup heavy cream
½ cup Grand Marnier
6 ounces butter

Combine chocolate, cream, and Grand Marnier in a heavy-bottomed saucepan. Heat over low heat until chocolate is melted and mixture is well combined. Add butter, one-quarter at a time, stirring continuously until glaze is combined, smooth, and shiny.

Warm Chocolate Pudding Cake

SERVES 6

I can't decide if this dessert is a cake or a pudding. What I AM sure of is that it is easy to make; and so warm and gooey, you'll want seconds.

5½ ounces bittersweet chocolate
11 tablespoons butter
3 eggs
3 egg yolks
⅔ cup sugar
5 tablespoons flour

Preheat oven to 325°. Butter and flour six 6-ounce custard cups.

Melt chocolate and butter in a double boiler or in microwave. Stir to combine and remove from heat.

Beat eggs, egg yolks, and sugar in a mixer for 10 minutes or until slightly thickened and pale. Mix in flour and chocolate mixture and beat until batter is thick and glossy. Divide among prepared cups.

Bake for 12 minutes or until edges are set and center moves slightly. Cool for 5 minutes. Unmold and serve with ice cream or whipped cream.

Tiramisu

SERVES 8

Someone once told me that you had to be Italian to make a good tiramisu. I told them all you need is some good rum and the strongest coffee you can find. And a good recipe, of course. I think this one is *deliciano*! What do you think?

¼ cup rum
½ cup strong old coffee or espresso
2 tablespoons cognac
16 to 20 ladyfingers
1 pound mascarpone cheese
2 eggs, separated
5 tablespoons confectioners' sugar
3 to 4 ounces semi-sweet chocolate, grated

Combine 2 tablespoons rum, coffee, and cognac in a small shallow bowl. Soak ladyfingers in mixture. Cover the bottom of a shallow 6-cup serving dish with soaked ladyfingers. Reserve.

In a separate bowl, beat together remaining rum, mascarpone, egg yolks, and sugar.

In a third bowl, beat egg whites until stiff but not dry. Fold whites into mascarpone mixture. Pour mixture over ladyfingers. Sprinkle with chocolate. Chill overnight. Serve cold.

Grand Marnier Zabaglione

YIELDS ABOUT 3 CUPS

The *Food Lovers' Companion* calls zabaglione "one of Italy's great gifts to the rest of the world." Considering all the Italian culinary contributions we enjoy, you'll have some understanding of how really wonderful this frothy dessert sauce is. It can be served alone or over fruit, cake, pastry, or ice cream. My favorite way? Over fresh picked summer berries.

5 egg yolks
8 tablespoons sugar
4 tablespoons Grand Marnier
1 cup heavy cream

Place egg yolks, 2 tablespoons sugar, and 2 tablespoons Grand Marnier in top of a double boiler set over simmering water. Beat for 20 minutes or until mixture is very thick and has doubled in volume.

Slowly add heavy cream and remaining sugar and Grand Marnier. Serve warm or cold.

Knock Down Bourbon Bread Pudding

SERVES 6

Traditional bread pudding is the ultimate comfort food, but try my spirited recipe if you want a bit of *Southern* comfort. I think it's time for a party.

5 cups stale bread cubes
3 large eggs
2 cups milk
¼ cup melted butter
1¼ cups sugar
1½ teaspoons vanilla
1¼ teaspoons nutmeg
1¼ teaspoons cinnamon
½ cup raisins or currants
¼ cup bourbon
Bourbon Sauce (see recipe)

Cover bottom of a 9 x 13-inch baking dish with bread cubes. Reserve.

Beat together all ingredients, except raisins and bourbon. Pour over bread. Sprinkle with raisins and bourbon and let stand for 20 minutes.

Press down bread to help absorb liquid and let stand 20 minutes more. Press again.

Bake in a preheated 350° oven for 45 to 60 minutes until custard is set. Serve warm with bourbon sauce.

Bourbon Sauce

1 tablespoon butter
½ cup sugar
½ cup bourbon
2 cups heavy cream
1 teaspoon cornstarch
2 teaspoons water

Heat butter and sugar in a medium saucepan over low heat.

When sugar starts to melt, remove from heat. Carefully add bourbon and let the alcohol burn off. (If bourbon ignites, just cover pan until flames go out.) Return pan to heat. Add cream and bring to a boil.

Combine cornstarch and water and stir in. Simmer until just thick enough to coat the back of a spoon. Serve warm.

Ricotta Cheese Pie

SERVES 6

I love cheesecake, especially this light Italian version that substitutes ricotta for cream cheese and incorporates the fresh flavors of orange and lemon.

3 cups ricotta cheese
¼ cup flour
2 tablespoons grated orange rind
2 tablespoons grated lemon rind
1 tablespoon vanilla
⅛ teaspoon salt
4 eggs
1 cup sugar
Flaky Pie Crust (see recipe)
Confectioners' sugar

Combine ricotta cheese, flour, rinds, vanilla, and salt in a large mixing bowl.

In a separate bowl, beat eggs until foamy. Gradually add sugar. Beat until soft peaks form. Add eggs to ricotta mixture and stir until well blended.

Reheat oven to 350°. Pour mixture into prebaked pie shell. Place dough strips on top of filling in a criss-cross pattern to form a lattice design.

Bake for 50 to 60 minutes or until filling is firm and pastry is golden brown. Let cool. Serve dusted with confectioners' sugar.

Flaky Pie Crust

2 cups flour
1 teaspoon salt
⅔ cup plus 2 tablespoons vegetable shortening
4 tablespoons cold water

Preheat oven to 350°.

Combine flour and salt. Use a pastry cutter or 2 knives to cut shortening into flour until lumps are pea size. Add water, 1 tablespoon at a time, mixing with a fork until flour is moist and dough holds together. Knead until combined but not overworked.

Divide dough in half. Gather one half of dough into a ball and roll out on a lightly floured work surface. Fit into a 9-inch pie plate. Bake in oven for 10 minutes.

Gather remaining dough into a ball and roll out on a lightly floured work surface. Cut into 1-inch-wide strips. Reserve.

Graham Cracker Crumb Crust

2 cups crushed graham crackers
½ cup butter, melted
3 tablespoons sugar
Pinch of salt
Pinch of cinnamon or nutmeg

Mix graham crumbs, butter, sugar, salt, and cinnamon until crumbs are evenly coated.

Press crumbs evenly against bottom and sides of a 9-inch pie pan. Refrigerate for 15 minutes.

Preheat oven to 350°. Bake for 10 minutes or until crisp and dry to the touch. Cool before adding filling.

Key Lime Pie

SERVES 6 TO 8

Small, round, and more yellow than green, Key limes can be hard to locate outside southern Florida; but don't worry if you can't find them or take a trip to Miami. You *can* make the pie with green limes or lemons. It won't be Key lime pie, but it will be fantastic.

- **4 egg yolks**
- **14 ounces sweetened condensed milk**
- **½ cup Key lime juice**
- **½ teaspoon cream of tartar**
- **1 9-inch baked Graham Cracker Crumb Crust (Recipe appears on page 103.)**
- **2 green limes**
- **1 cup water**
- **½ cup sugar**
- **2 cups heavy cream**
- **4 tablespoons confectioners' sugar**
- **1 teaspoon vanilla**

Preheat oven to 325°.

Beat egg yolks until thickened and pale. Add condensed milk and mix on low speed. Add ¼ cup lime juice and cream of tartar and mix. Add remaining juice and mix. Pour into baked pie shell.

Bake for 10 to 15 minutes or until center is firm and dry to touch. Cool and refrigerate for 3 hours.

Use a zester to remove strips of rind from the limes. Blanch strips in boiling water for 5 minutes; then drain. Refresh under cold water and drain again.

Combine 1 cup water and sugar in a saucepan. Heat over medium heat until water begins to simmer. Allow water to simmer for 5 minutes. Add lime peels. Cook, stirring often, for about 10 minutes or until peels are translucent. Remove pan from heat and allow peels to cool in syrup.

Combine heavy cream, confectioners' sugar, and vanilla in a chilled bowl. Whip until cream holds a soft shape.

Garnish pie with whipped cream and candied lime slices.

Bananas Flambé

SERVES 4

Legend has it that the original Bananas Foster was created in 1950 at the legendary Brennan's Restaurant in New Orleans. Every chef experiments with this classic dish, but banana lovers like me know ... it's all about the bananas, so go crazy.

2 tablespoons butter
2 tablespoons brown sugar
4 bananas, peeled and sliced crosswise
¼ teaspoon ground cinnamon
¼ cup dark rum
¼ cup crème de banane
1 pint vanilla or chocolate ice cream or frozen yogurt

Combine butter and brown sugar in a skillet. Cook over medium heat until mixture forms a syrup, about 3 minutes. Add banana slices and cinnamon and sauté for 3 minutes.

Gently turn slices to coat with syrup. Add rum and crème de banane. Remove pan from heat. Carefully ignite liquor with a lit match. Allow flame to subside and cook 1 minute more.

Scoop ice cream into serving bowls. Spoon bananas and syrup over ice cream and dig in.

Sweet Potato Crème Brûlée

SERVES 8

Although sweet potatoes can be cooked just like potatoes, these aren't your average spuds. After all, the name is "sweet." The taste is supreme.

3½ cups heavy cream
2 cups sugar
5 eggs
1¾ cups sweet potato puree
1 teaspoon vanilla
1½ teaspoons cinnamon
1 teaspoon ginger
½ teaspoon nutmeg
¼ teaspoon ground cloves
3 tablespoons bourbon or rum
½ cup dark brown sugar

Preheat oven to 350°. Place eight 6-ounce soufflé dishes or ramekins in a roasting pan. Fill pan with water to reach about half way up the sides of dishes.

Combine cream and sugar in a saucepan. Cook, stirring often, over medium heat until sugar dissolves. Reserve.

Beat eggs in a mixing bowl until pale yellow. Beat in sweet potato puree, vanilla, cinnamon, ginger, nutmeg, cloves, and bourbon. Gradually stir in hot cream mixture. Strain and pour into soufflé dishes. Bake for 1 hour. Remove dishes from pan and refrigerate until thoroughly chilled or overnight.

Preheat broiler. Sprinkle brown sugar over custard. Brown under broiler until sugar is caramelized but not burned. Serve immediately or chill.

Chocolate Chip Sweet Potato Cannoli

SERVES 6

South Philly is cannoli heaven. People wait in long, long lines at Italian bakeries just to get a half dozen of these pastries. With this recipe you can easily make them at home and skip the lines. Fuggettabouit.

- **2 cups ricotta cheese**
- **2 cups peeled and cooked sweet potatoes (about 3 large)**
- **¼ cup sugar**
- **3 tablespoons amaretto**
- **½ cup semi-sweet chocolate chips**
- **2 prebaked cannoli shells (available at most grocery stores)**

Combine cheese, sweet potatoes, sugar, and amaretto in a food processor. Process until smooth. Refrigerate for 1 hour or until stiff. Fold in chocolate chips. Fill cannoli shells with mixture and serve.

Sweet Potato Chocolate Ravioli
with Pecan Bourbon Sauce

SERVES 2

Now this is fusion! The quintessential Southern staple packed into a classic Italian presentation and topped with Louisiana's favorite dessert sauce.

4 ounces semi-sweet chocolate
1 cup heavy cream
1 packet (2 ounces) unflavored gelatin
½ cup hot water
1 large sweet potato
2 tablespoons butter, softened
½ cup sugar
¼ teaspoon cinnamon
¼ teaspoon nutmeg
¼ teaspoon salt
½ cup ricotta cheese
Pecan Bourbon Sauce (see recipe)

Combine chocolate and heavy cream in a small saucepan. Warm over medium heat until chocolate melts. Remove from heat. Dissolve unflavored gelatin in hot water. Add to chocolate-cream mixture and stir to combine.

Cover a cookie sheet pan with plastic wrap. Pour mixture into pan and spread to approximately 1/8-inch thick. Chill in refrigerator for 30 minutes.

Boil sweet potato until fork tender, about 15 minutes. Drain, cool, and peel. Combine butter, sugar, cinnamon, nutmeg, and salt in a bowl. Add sweet potato and mash to combine. Fold in ricotta cheese.

Remove chocolate from refrigerator and cut into 2-inch squares. Place 1 teaspoon sweet potato filling in the center of a square. Cover with another square and crimp edges together. Continue process with remaining squares. Refrigerate until ready to serve. Smother with pecan bourbon sauce.

Pecan Bourbon Sauce

¼ cup sugar
1 cup heavy cream
¼ cup halved pecans
Bourbon to taste (I use about 2 ounces.)

Combine sugar, heavy cream, pecans, and bourbon in a saucepan. Cook over medium heat until mixture reduces by one-quarter. Serve hot or cold over ravioli.

Pecan Bar Cookies

YIELDS ABOUT 75 COOKIES

I just can't leave well enough alone, so sometimes I melt chocolate and drizzle it over these bars . . . the more decadent the better!

- **1¼ cups plus 3 tablespoons sifted flour**
- **½ teaspoon baking powder**
- **¾ cup firmly packed dark brown sugar**
- **½ cup butter**
- **2 eggs**
- **1 teaspoon vanilla**
- **¾ cup dark corn syrup**
- **3 cups pecan halves**

Preheat oven to 350°. Butter a 10 x 15-inch jelly-roll pan.

Mix 1¼ cups flour, baking powder, and ½ cup brown sugar in a food processor. Cut in butter slowly, turning machine off and on until mixture resembles fine meal. Press mixture against bottom of prepared pan to form a smooth layer (crust).

Beat together remaining flour and sugar, eggs, vanilla, and corn syrup until smooth. Pour mixture over crust and spread evenly. Top with pecan halves.

Bake for 35 to 40 minutes or until golden. Cool in pan for 15 minutes. Run knife around edges of pan to loosen cookie and invert onto a baking sheet. Remove pan and place rack over cookie. Turn cookie and rack over and cool. (To make cutting easier, freeze cookie for 30 minutes.) Cut into 1 x 2-inch bars.

Chewy Pralines

YIELDS APPROXIMATELY 60 COOKIES.

Visit New Orleans and you'll fall in love with pralines. You have no choice! These sweet cookie-candies are made in countless street-side stores, and there's no ignoring their seductive aroma or addictive taste. Make this recipe once, and you'll be hooked too.

1 quart heavy cream
1 pound dark brown sugar
3 cups chopped toasted pecans

Combine cream and brown sugar in a heavy saucepan over medium heat. Simmer for 1 hour or until a candy thermometer reaches 270°.

Reduce heat and cook down until mixture becomes "chewy" and a spoonful dropped into ice water hardens. Stir in pecans.

Drop candy by tablespoonfuls onto wax paper. Let cool.

TIDBITS AND BISCUITS

France's Cheese Biscuits

YIELDS APPROXIMATELY 24 BISCUITS

I can remember making these biscuits with my mother. We never wrote down the recipe, so we had to reconfigure it every time we made it. I guess that was part of the fun. Serve with stew, turkey soup, or alone with butter and honey.

- **2 cups sifted flour**
- **½ teaspoon baking powder**
- **½ teaspoon baking soda**
- **1 cup grated Parmesan cheese**
- **1 teaspoon salt**
- **½ teaspoon black pepper**
- **4 tablespoons cold butter, diced**
- **1 cup cold milk (You can substitute buttermilk for added flavor.)**

Preheat oven to 350º. Combine all dry ingredients. Cut in butter, using a pastry cutter or two knives, until mixture resembles coarse crumbs. Gradually add milk and knead gently. Do not overwork or biscuits will become tough.

Transfer dough to a lightly floured work surface. Roll to ½-inch thick. Cut out biscuits with a 2-inch biscuit cutter. Repeat, without overworking dough, until all dough is used.

Place biscuits 2 inches apart on an ungreased cookie sheet. Bake for 20 minutes or until light golden brown and almost double in height.

Joe Brown's Beignets

Beignets are the official doughnuts of Louisiana! Walk around the French Quarter, and you're bound to see people covered with powdered sugar. Chances are they were snacking on beignets from the famous Café Du Monde. Similar to a fritter, beignets can be savory or sweet, as in this recipe.

2 cups flour
1 tablespoon baking powder
1 teaspoon cinnamon
1 teaspoon salt
2 eggs
¾ cup milk
¼ cup sugar
½ teaspoon vanilla extract
Vegetable oil
1 cup confectioners' sugar

Sift together flour, baking powder, cinnamon, and salt into a large mixing bowl. Cover and set aside.

In a separate bowl, beat together eggs, milk, sugar, and vanilla extract. Pour wet ingredients into dry ingredients and stir to form dough.

Turn dough out onto a lightly floured work surface. Knead until smooth and elastic, about 3 to 4 minutes. Roll dough out to a ¼-inch-thick circle. Slice diagonally to form 3-inch-tall diamonds.

Fill deep fryer with enough oil to completely cover beignets. Heat to 375°. (If oil smokes, reduce to 350°.) Fry beignets in oil, a few at a time, turning once, until golden brown. Remove with a slotted spoon and drain well on paper towels.

Smother with confectioners' sugar and serve warm with a good cup of coffee.

Dark Roux

Ask a dozen Louisiana folks how to cook and they'll all give you the same advice ... "First ya make a roux." Roux is made from cooked flour and fat and is the basis of many soups, stews, gravies, and gumbos in Cajun and Creole cookery. It thickens (with no lumps!) and adds flavor too. Dark roux has an intense flavor, a wonderful roasted nutty taste, but tends to have less thickening power than blond roux.

1 cup soy oil
¾ cup flour

Heat oil in a heavy-bottomed saucepan over high heat. Stir in flour and reduce to medium-low. Stir, every few minutes, with a wooden spoon until it reaches a peanut butter consistency and is dark brown. This may take up to 1 hour. Make sure it doesn't burn. Use your eyes and nose; watch and smell – you'll know if it's getting too hot. Store leftovers in refrigerator for up to 2 months.

YIELDS 1½ CUPS

Blond Roux

Roux comes in several shades from off-white to dark brown, depending on how long you cook it. Creole cooks tend to prefer a blond or medium roux for gumbos, where Cajun cooks usually prefer a very dark roux, which is wonderfully smoky tasting. I use both blond roux or dark roux, depending on the dish and my patience.

1 cup soy oil
¾ cup flour

Heat oil in a heavy-bottomed saucepan over high heat. Stir in flour and reduce to medium-low. Stir, every few minutes, with a wooden spoon until it reaches a warm honey color. This will take from 5 to 10 minutes. Watch so that it doesn't burn. Store leftovers in refrigerator for up to 2 months.

YIELDS 1½ CUPS

Joe's Cajun Seasoning

3 tablespoons garlic powder
2½ tablespoons paprika
2 tablespoons salt
1 tablespoon black pepper
1 tablespoon cayenne pepper
1 tablespoon onion powder
1 tablespoon ground oregano
1 tablespoon ground thyme

Combine all ingredients. Store in an airtight container in a cool, dry place. Shake or stir to recombine before each use. Seasoning can be stored for up to 3 months.

Index

PEOPLE
HAPPY

EAT
AT
JOE'S

EAT AT JOE'S

N

O

P

R

S

EAT
AT
JOE'S

T

V

W

Z

The end!

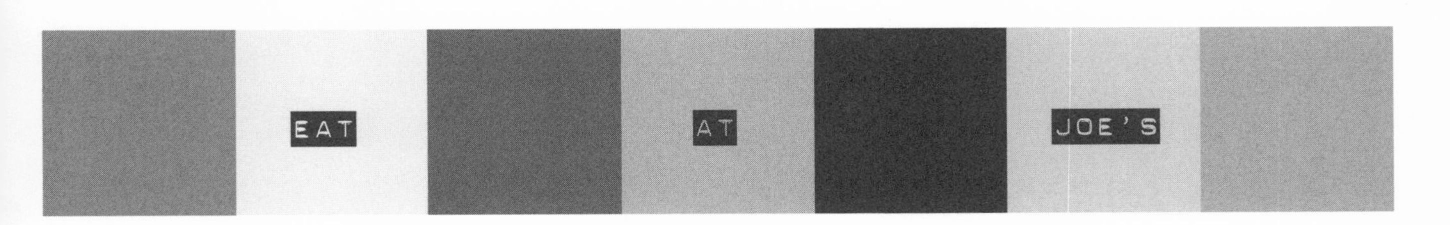

Order Form

Please send me ________ copies of *Joe Brown's Melange Cafe Cookbook* at $14.95 per copy.

__________ Book amount total

__________ Sales tax: New Jersey addresses, please add $.90 per book

__________ Shipping: $2.50 for first book; $1 for each additional book

__________ Total amount enclosed

Name ____

Address ____

City/State/ZIP ______________________________________

Phone ____________________ E-Mail ____________________

Credit Card # ________________ Exp. _____ Name on Card ____________

Checks, money orders, and credit cards (American Express, Novis, Visa, and MasterCard) are accepted for payment.

By Fax: Fax this order form to 856-663-9493
By E-mail: Write to chefjoebrown@msn.com
By Mail: Mail this order form to: Melange Cafe
Book Processing
1601 Chapel Avenue
Cherry Hill, NJ 08002

Gift copies and corporate packages are available! Call for details.

About the Author

Joe Brown, executive chef and owner of Melange Cafe, Cherry Hill, NJ, was born to feed a crowd.

The youngest of ten children, Joe learned to cook at his mother's side at a young age. "My mother was from Tennessee and really knew how to cook, and there were a lot of people to cook for," says Brown. "I liked helping her in the kitchen and just sort of fell in love with cooking."

This early love of cooking led him on a self-propelled culinary adventure. Formal training was received at The Restaurant School in Philadelphia and through work at local New Jersey restaurants, but trips to New Orleans really sparked Joe's obsession with Louisiana-style cooking and led him to open Melange Cafe in 1995. At Melange, Southern hospitality plus the passion of Italy and the heat of Louisiana are always on the menu.

Joe lives with his wife Robin and son Jordan in Voorhees, NJ.